Can I Quote You on That?

A practical handbook
for company executives who deal with the media

William Essex

Hh Harriman House Publishing

HARRIMAN HOUSE LTD
43 Chapel Street
Petersfield
Hampshire
GU32 3DY

Tel: +44 (0)1730 233870
Fax: +44 (0)1730 233880

First published in Great Britain in 2006
Copyright © Papernet Limited

The right of William Essex to be identified as Author has been asserted in accordance with the Copyright, Design and Patents Act 1988

ISBN: 1-8975-9789-4
ISBN 13: 978-1897597-89-7

British Library Cataloguing in Publication Data
A CIP catalogue record for this book can be obtained from the British Library.

Printed and bound in Great Britain by Biddles Ltd, Kings Lynn, Norfolk
Index by Indexing Specialists (UK) Ltd.

Contents

Biography

William Essex is a freelance journalist, writer and occasional broadcaster who also trains executives to deal with the media. He has experience on both sides of the camera, microphone, notepad and digital recording device, and likes to believe that dealing with the media successfully need not be a stressful experience. You just need to know what they want and how to provide it in a way that also delivers what you want. That's the idea behind this book.

William Essex is married with four children and now lives in Cornwall. He divides his time between his family, the media outlets for which he writes, and the companies whose executives he prepares for media contact.

Preface

Who the book is for

This book is written for CEOs, board-level directors, heads of department, entrepreneurs, managers, bankers, lawyers, accountants, financial advisers; in fact, for executives at every level in every line of business whose responsibilities include dealing with journalists. It is intended to be useful both for first-timers with the media, and for those looking to fine-tune their journalist-handling skills. Its objective is to provide a set of techniques that can be applied to any media contact, based on an understanding of what journalists want and why they want it. The reader of this book will be equipped both to meet journalists' needs in ways that achieve the right coverage from any given interview, and to form long-term, mutually beneficial media relationships.

What the book covers

Can I Quote You on That? starts at your first contact with the media, whether this comes as an unexpected phone call from a trade journalist, or as a long-arranged interview, or in the form of an email from your PR department to say that you're booked on breakfast television tomorrow morning. It starts with some advice on how to react to unexpected media contact, then moves on to discuss how to prepare what you want to say in an interview, so that the journalist will find it usable. The book talks you through the various interview experiences you might have, with both the print and broadcast media, and then discusses whether, and if so how, to follow up an interview. There's a lengthy chapter on crisis management, and then, just in case, some advice on your legal rights and how to use them.

How the book is structured

The book begins with The Emergency Pages, which take the place of the conventional executive summary. They are for quick reference if, say, a journalist has turned up in reception, or is about to be put through, or if the camera crew is already setting up in your office.

After that, Chapter 1 focuses on preparing for the media. Simple advice, but often overlooked; do read it. Chapter 2 gets into the detail of what journalists want and why they want it. You know what you want to get out of any interview, but you'll be unlikely to get it unless you think through the reasons why you might have been contacted. Journalists have a job to do, and it isn't taking dictation.

Then Chapter 3 describes techniques for preparing what you want to say in a journalist-friendly style that should ensure coverage. Chapter 4 takes you through the interview experience itself, in whatever form it might take, and Chapter 5 prepares you for the varieties of broadcast interview that you might encounter. Chapter 6 is worth reading if you're struck with a post-interview urge to call the journalist and talk some more.

Crisis management is covered in Chapter 7. It's in the nature of a crisis not only that it's serious and comes at a bad time, but also that it can get a lot worse if the media aren't handled well. Chapter 7 suggests a media-oriented crisis-management strategy that you might want to put in place now, and also offers step-by-step advice on how to manage a live crisis. Then, in Chapter 8, we discuss your legal rights vis-à-vis the media.

Supporting website

A website supporting this book can be found at:

www.harriman-house.com/caniquoteyou

Introduction

Media contact is a fact of business life. Sooner or later, if you're getting ahead with your career, you'll start to get calls from the media. Perhaps that's already happening. There are trade magazines, newsletters, newspapers, breakfast shows, business programmes, TV and radio news, online media, etc. They're all staffed by journalists hunting for people who can provide comments, opinions, interviews, sound bites and quotes. If you can give them what they want, in the way they want it, they'll return the favour by giving you a raised profile in the long term and access to editorial space for your news and views. Your colleagues and customers will get accustomed to seeing your name in print and your face on screen. Your business will benefit.

Whatever your position and whoever's calling, this book gives you a proven strategy for getting the best out of your contacts with journalists. Like most things, it's not rocket science. But there are ways of handling the media that work effectively for both sides. And there are ways that don't. Journalists have a job to do, and wasting time on people who don't understand what they need is not part of it. So this book will identify what journalists need from you, why they need it and what they do with it. Then we'll talk about delivering what you want to say, in a way that fits in with those needs. We'll discuss the differences and similarities between print, television and radio. We'll also talk about forming long-term relationships with journalists, so that they come to regard you as a valuable contact.

This book is based on a media training course that was launched in 1998 as a sideline by two full-time journalists and has been running regularly ever since. We've trained newly appointed CEOs, board-level directors, whole management teams, marketing departments, bankers, stockbrokers, fund managers, entrepreneurs, lawyers, accountants, dot-com people and, so far, one restaurant owner. It's a practical course, with an emphasis on doing rather than theorising, and it's based on experience from both sides of the microphone and the camera. We've answered just about every question that could be asked about journalists, on everything from quote approval to crisis management, and those answers form the backbone of this book.

This is not a book about hiring a PR company to raise your media profile. Nor does it tell you how to write a press release, or where to send one. This book starts at your first contact with the media. If a trade journalist wants to come in and interview you for a feature, or the marketing director bursts into your office with the good news that you're booked on breakfast television tomorrow morning, or Radio 4 invites you to join the panel for a phone-in programme this afternoon, this book is all about what to do next.

You can handle the media without putting yourself through a full-scale media training course first, and it's probably not a good idea to keep a journalist on hold until you've finished this book. But if you want to find out, from your own experience, what you could gain from handling the media really well, read on.

William Essex

Acknowledgements

I'd like to thank Gaynor Drew for her help with research in the early stages. We began by going through Bookwise, Amazon, Ottakar's and a variety of other databases, and found that there's no other book like this on the market. There are books on management, books on marketing, books on communications and books on customer-relationship management, but nothing that focuses exclusively on dealing with journalists. A good start.

I'd also like to thank Hugh Fraser, who's a full-time journalist as well as my media-training partner, and Aisling Lee, TV producer and cameraperson, who not only operates the cameras, lights, cables and connections when we're doing TV training, but also knows everything there is to be known about looking good on screen. Together we're insidertraining.net, and we've been preparing business people for the media since 1998.

Particular thanks also to Neil Boom at Gresham PR Limited and John Norris at Moonlight Media. Key players in this business also include Mike Lord, Roland Cross, Henry Gewanter at Positive Profile, Laura Hastings and Terry Hepplewhite. Thanks also to Steve Falla, Mike Sunier, Paul Ham, Stephen Spurdon, Andy Webb and Andrew Waterworth. This list would be longer, but some people spoke off the record and others chose to remind me that insidertraining.net doesn't disclose the names of clients. You know who you are: thank you.

Author's note

This is a book about journalists. Most of it applies equally well to print journalists, radio journalists, television journalists and indeed online journalists, except where it's made obvious that it doesn't. Also, I have used a variety of terms – story, feature, article, package, et cetera – to describe what journalists produce. These terms are interchangeable, except where they're not. I have referred to journalists variously as "he", "she" and "they", which seems more consistent with reality than just using "they" throughout.

The Emergency Pages

Introduction

Because this is a book about handling the media, we have The Emergency Pages instead of an executive summary. They are designed for use if your phone call, interview or TV appearance is imminent, and have been divided into three sections: print, TV and radio. Then we talk about handling phone messages from journalists, and finally, we get onto what happens after your interview.

If you have time, some of the points in the Print section can be applied equally well to TV and radio. If you don't, the TV and radio sections cover everything you need to get through a broadcast interview at short notice. There is some overlap between the TV and radio sections, but that's inevitable; key points are necessarily repeated.

Everything said here is repeated at greater length, and explained in greater detail, later in the book. For now, hold the thought that media contact is almost always a good thing, and even when it isn't, you can improve the situation by handling it correctly. Read quickly, and good luck.

Covered in this section:

- Print

- Television

- Radio

- Returning calls

- After the interview

- And finally … what happens in a successful interview?

Print

If you really have got a journalist on hold, or waiting in the outer office, glance through the bits in bold. But do it quickly. Journalists don't like to wait.*

If you have a couple of minutes, here, in order of importance, is what you do, and what you don't do, immediately.

1   If you think you know what this is going to be about, scribble down a few bullet-point headings. Things you'd like to get across. Give yourself about three seconds for this. If nothing comes, don't worry about it.

2   **Pick up the phone or go out and get them**. Do whatever comes naturally, but it's better to be personal from the start. Ideally, don't send somebody else. Don't be finishing another meeting as they're brought in, unless you want them wondering what it was about when they're supposed to be listening to you.

3   **Apologise for keeping them waiting**. Even if you didn't. A lot of journalists think they're important. Act as though you do too.

4   **Ask, "What do you need?"** You can also ask, "When's your deadline?", but better not to unless you're going to have to delay doing the interview until later. "Who else have you interviewed?" is another no-no.

5   **Listen to the answer.** If you're lucky, you can circle a couple of your bullet points. Or you can scribble down some bullet points now.

6   **Never, ever, say that you'll think about it** and come back with some thoughts later. As soon as they put the phone down on you, they're going to call the next person on their list of contacts.

7   If you absolutely have to, and not otherwise, **ask them to tell you more about the publication**, more about the piece they're writing, et cetera. Journalists hate having to do this, but it's a way of giving yourself time to think.

8   If you absolutely have to, and not otherwise, ask for **quote approval** now rather than later.

9   **They only want to hear what they've asked you to tell them.**

10 And they want to hear it now. This is where you **deliver what they need**.

11 **So say something quotable**. Make it punchy, opinionated and relevant, in that order. Make it short. Not necessarily controversial, but you'll come over better if you say what you think rather than try to express some kind of company line.

*And as they sit in your reception area, they might be inspired to start composing a short filler piece on horrible office furniture.

12 **Stop.** Wait for the next question. They just need the answer. Not the background. Not the history of the industry. Just a short, quotable answer.

13 Assume **they already know the parts they're not asking about**.

14 **Don't fill silences.** If the next question doesn't come immediately, wait for it. You'd be surprised at the number of people who feel compelled to keep on talking if there's a silence.

15 **Don't answer the question, "Why?"** If you've just given the perfect answer, but the journalist just says "Why?" and then waits, the idea is to knock you off your prepared script. The question means it's time to loosen up, not to flannel around trying to make your answer clearer and in the process saying something you didn't want to say.

16 Don't sell. This is not an opportunity to promote your company. The benefit will come indirectly. You're being quoted because you're an authority, right? The reader will get that subliminal message.

17 **Speak in short, complete sentences.** They'll take quotes and sound bites from what you say. But they can't take sound bites beginning "...and another thing about that is ..." To quote that, they'd have to reword it, which means you might be misquoted.

18 **Use colourful, specific, visual language as far as possible.** "One in ten people" is better than "Ten per cent of the population." Examples and anecdotes are good, if short.

19 **Don't refer back to the last time you met, or to the literature you gave them last time.** They've been writing about other stuff since, and they've probably forgotten it. Assume they'll only use the quotes you give them this time.

20 **Journalists love case histories**. If you have clients who would be willing to be written up as case histories, say so.

21 If you've got graphs, charts, mugshots, statistics, anything else that might break up the page, offer it. And deliver it. **The budget may not run to much illustration**.

22 **Don't mention the money you spend on advertising.** It's just embarrassing.

23 **Write down any promises you make. Be very literal-minded about keeping them.** If you say later today, tomorrow morning isn't good enough. They'll have given up and called somebody else.

24 At the end of the interview, any competent journalist will ask, "Is there anything I've missed, or anything else you'd like to add?" The correct answer is no, the journalist has done a very good job, asked all the right questions, and **in case there's anything else, here's my business card**.

25 Afterwards, **make sure you're available**. If you're not there to confirm a crucial detail at the last minute, like the correct placing of the commas in your job title, they may not be able to use your quote.

Television

By the time a TV crew has set up cameras, lights, microphones, et cetera, in your office, the chances are that you will be as unnerved as if you had just stumbled into a TV studio full of cameras, lights, disembodied voices from the control room above, people looking busy and cables to trip over. So we'll start with two brief suggestions on how to control your likely state of mind.

1   **Don't panic.** Take a deep breath. Turn off your mobile phone. Check your shoelaces, zips, buttons. If there's a mirror (and some people bring little mirrors) check that you're not wearing breakfast on your chin. Do your expenses. Teach yourself to juggle paperclips. Do anything to distract yourself. Above all, do not rehearse the answers you're about to give. They should be spontaneous rather than an attempt to repeat what sounded good a moment ago.

2   Remember that **television is a lot easier than radio**. All you have to do is speak and sound interesting. You don't even have to answer the question you're asked. As long as you keep talking.

3   If you're being interviewed in your office, **check your background.** The rubber plant would look better beside you than immediately behind your head.

4   Television audiences judge by **appearance and tone of voice**. It is just possible that some people will remember what you say. But it is more likely that they will take away an impression that you are, let's say, an approachable-looking person who obviously knows the subject and with whom it would be pleasant to do business. Don't try too hard, but whatever you're saying, say it with authority.

5   Apart from sounding and looking good, your other big objective is to **check that they've got your name and company name right**, both when they introduce you and on the caption. If they introduce you wrongly, start your first answer by correcting them. Do it good-humouredly. It's not a big deal, but you want to get it right. Say your company name clearly (even if you're only correcting your own name).

6   When you're asked a question in a live television interview, pause for a split second, a very split second, and then say something. It would be nice if you answered the question, but **the only thing that really matters to the TV people is that you talk**. Be authoritative, et cetera, as above. (There's more on this matter of pausing in the Radio section below, where it really matters.)

7   In a recorded interview, **speak in complete sentences**, with small pauses between them. If you fumble an answer, or fill it up with ums and ahs, stop, pause, start again. The pauses are useful for editing.

8   Remember to **stop when you've given your answer**, and always stop if the interviewer is trying to ask another question. It doesn't look good to drone on and on, and if you've given your answer, it's the interviewer's problem if there's a silence.

9   **Don't sell**. Nobody's interested in hearing that your company's wonderful. They'll cut you short, or not use you at all. And you'll never hear from them again.

Radio

You're in the studio, or on the phone, or facing a microphone in your office. The interview is about to start.

1   **Ask questions**. What's your angle? What do you want me to say? What aspect are you most interested in? Get the detail straight in your mind: what do they want?

2   While you're asking questions, **don't rehearse your answers**. Each answer should be spontaneous rather than an attempt to repeat what sounded good a second ago.

3   Whether the interview is live or recorded, when you're asked the first question, **pause for a split second**. A very split second. Practically no time at all. Subconsciously, by doing this, you take control. A secondary benefit is that you immediately get the attention of everybody listening. Silence on the radio scares the radio people and gets the attention of the audience. But don't play silent just for that reason.

4   **In a live radio interview, just talk.** You don't have any obligation to answer the question you're asked. But you must sound confident, relaxed, expert, approachable. The radio audience, who matter much more than the person asking the questions, will judge you almost entirely by the tone of your voice.

5   **In a recorded interview, speak in complete sentences**. After each complete point you make, pause very slightly. If you fumble an answer, or start a sentence with a sequence of ums and ahs, stop, pause, start again. Each pause is a flat line on the computer screen when they come to edit the tape. Easy to see where to cut.

6   **Don't go on too long.** When you've made your point, and added the thing that occurred to you while you were making it, stop.

7   **Always stop if the interviewer shows signs of wanting to ask another question**. You might be interested in what you're saying, but you've lost your audience.

8   **Don't sell**. Don't go on about how wonderful your company is. You will come across as boring, and so insensitive that you're not going to answer the perfectly reasonable question you've just been asked. If it's live, they'll cut you off. If it's recorded, they won't use it.

Returning calls

If the emergency is a Post-it Note on your desk saying that a journalist called five minutes ago and could you call back, **do it now**. No journalist sets out to research a feature with just one possible interviewee. If you don't take the call, the journalist will go to the second name on the list of possible contacts. You may have missed the call but you've still got to get in first.

For this reason, it is sensible to **establish a system whereby you are notified of media calls as they happen**. If you're in the habit of returning calls at the end of the working day, you will spend a lot of time talking to journalists who might listen to you out of politeness, but who will almost certainly have got what they want from somebody else.

The bigger the opportunity, the more this is true. **They won't hold the front page because you're in a board meeting**, any more than the TV news will be delayed half an hour because you're not back from lunch.

After the interview

There is only one moment in life when you are absolutely one hundred percent ready and eager to do an interview, a broadcast interview in particular, and that is immediately after you've done one. You're still fired up with the stress of it all (and if you've just done television, you're probably still wearing the make-up).

Use this. **Now is the moment to write notes about what worked** and what didn't work. Now is the moment to call your PR adviser with wild schemes for global media domination. Now is the moment to write your own media-handling memo for yourself and the people back at the office. The feeling will wear off, but right now, you could give a memorable interview to just about anybody on just about anything.

Unless you blew the whole thing. It happens sometimes. If that really happened, and you're not mistaken (a good interview can feel as though it went badly), don't play it back in your mind. Write the notes. Talk to your PR people. Their whole professional life is taken up with getting people to perform well in front of journalists. They might suggest media training, or they might just take you back to the office, stick you in front of a video recorder, and ask you difficult questions until you get the sound bites right.

Everybody can handle the media. It just takes practice. So treat every interview as a learning experience, and get ready for the next one.

And finally ... what happens in a successful interview?

You get a chance to put yourself, your product and/or your company in front of the buying public. **Because this is an interview, and not an advertisement, you're taken that little bit more seriously.** You come across as an expert. People get the message that you want to put across.

The interviewer gets three things out of a successful interview. **First, there are the quotes/sound bites you give her.** These make the end result more authoritative and more interesting, while also demonstrating to the folk back at the office that the interviewer actually has gone out and done some research. Secondly, out of the parts of your interview that she doesn't quote, the interviewer gets what she needs to sound as though she knows what she's talking about.

And thirdly, the interviewer gets **a name to put in her contact book**. Next time she gets to do a piece on this subject, because she knows that you can deliver the goods, she'll call you first and not your rival.

The rest of this book is about delivering perfect interviews every time. For now, remember those three things: getting taken seriously; giving quotes and knowledge; getting called next time.

Also remember that the result of a perfect interview is not just the coverage you get this time, but the opportunity to get more coverage next time. If you're good, they'll call you again and again.

1

Preparing For The Media

Introduction

This chapter is mostly about attitudes and expectations. There are some not-so-minor details to discuss, and some significant practical points to be addressed as well. But mostly, preparing for media contact means understanding who these people are and what you can expect from them.

Dealing with the media is not like dealing with customers, prospective customers, salespeople, rivals, colleagues or indeed just about anybody else. It is true to say, and you can count on being told this by any PR professional you might decide to hire, that journalists are, after all, just people with a job to do. But if you're new to the media, you can bet that the same PR person will go from describing journalists as just people, to recommending that you embark on an expensive media-training course to learn how to deal with them.

Expensive media training or not, before you send out your first press release, or meet your first journalist, you will almost certainly be encouraged to rehearse your answers to the questions you want to answer, and more importantly, to the questions you want to avoid. You will be advised to prepare one or two, possibly three, points that you want to get across, and you will be told that the best way to handle your opportunity to project your company and its products to the media and the public, is NOT to go on about your product or your company. You might be warned never to dodge or refuse to answer an unwelcome question, and you might even hear the phrase, "Journalists never forgive and never forget" (see below).

By the time you get to the end of the preparation process, there's a fair chance that you'll be startled when you find that your first journalist is actually human. You'll be surprised that the questions seem to be friendly, and with any luck, you'll relax enough to deliver a coherent series of answers that contain the points you want to make. But then, when the story comes out, there's also a fair chance that you'll be disappointed with the amount of coverage you're given. The journalist hasn't used your interview in the way you wanted it to be used. Worse, a rival of yours has been quoted making one of the points you wanted to make.

Here's what you'll be told next:

- Journalists are just people. Yes, they're human.

- They don't (shouldn't) play favourites, but they interview a lot of people, and enough of those interviews go well enough for them not to worry too much about the rest.

- They don't owe you a quote. Not every time, anyway.

- They're not doing you a favour by interviewing you.

- They've got a job to do. Unfortunately, that job is not writing down what you want to say, and then quoting you saying it.

- Anyway, the interview you've just done doesn't matter. What matters is the long-term relationship with the journalist.

You might also be reminded that handling the media is a competitive business and a lot of people do it very well. There might even be some tactful comments along the lines of, "Perhaps you could have spent less time bringing the conversation back round to the company." Or even, "Perhaps you should have let her interrupt with a question every now and then."

But even after all that, maybe you'll still have a slight doubt at the back of your mind: you're sure the interview went well; was there something else that wasn't quite right? Pity you kept her waiting so long in reception, with nothing to read but last year's annual report, but you did explain that you had to take that important call … didn't you?

This whole book is about getting the coverage you want from the contacts you have with the media. This chapter is about getting it right from the start. Journalists are, as we've said, human. But they're unusual human beings, in that they're doing a job that is unlike any other. They are also important humans, in that they can connect you to large numbers of potential customers. They can raise your company's profile and they can make you and your company look good.

And it's free.

So let's talk about getting it right from the start.

Covered in this chapter:

- How it's done, and how it's done well

- How it's done badly by invitation

- "Journalists never forgive and never forget"

- What do we know so far?

- You're very interesting

- Read yourself in

- Now you've hit the middle-sized time, look after the juniors

- In-house and external PR agencies

- Paying for PR

- Freebies, jollies, lunches, cuddly toys and contact numbers

- We are *not* talking about advertising here

- And finally … the media-friendly enterprise

How it's done, and how it's done well

First, how it's done. We'll take this from the journalist's point of view.

So you're a journalist. You've got a story to research. Therefore, you have a list of possible contacts. Some of these are people you've interviewed before, some are names from the bottom of press releases, some came from PR houses and some you found when you Googled the subject of your story.

You don't know much about your subject yet (or at least, your knowledge isn't up to date), although you've scribbled out a few possible questions to get an interview started, based on something you read on a website, and you need people to quote. You could call the people you always call, but everybody uses them and it's high time you got yourself some new names.

You punch in the first number on your list. A recorded voice asks you to press one for sales. Your call is valuable to this company, but even so, you put the phone down, cross out the name, and try the second number.

A voice answers. Switchboard. You ask for the contact name. What's it concerning? You explain (you should have rehearsed this). The phone goes dead. Then a voice says, "Press office". You have to explain again. The voice says she'll see what availability your contact has. The phone goes dead.

Then one of two things happens:

1   The press-office voice comes back on the line. Can she get back to you with a time? In the meantime, could you email over the questions you want to ask?

2   Another voice comes on the line. It's the contact's PA. You have to run through the explanation again. Definitely should have rehearsed this. Hm. Your contact

is very busy. Can she get back to you? In the meantime, could you email over the questions you want to ask?

You agree to email over questions. But if you get lucky with any of the other possible contacts on your list, you won't have to bother. You decide to leave that until last.

You ring the next number. This time, you ask for the press office, but that's the wrong move. The guy wants the list of questions and some details of the publication and yeah, you'll do all that if you have to. But time is passing and you're getting nowhere and ringing another number would be a lot quicker than getting into his bureaucracy.

So you scroll down your list to a number that looks as though it might be a direct line and call it. You're straight through to the PA. But the contact is on holiday this week and there's nobody else in the *entire* organisation who is authorised to comment on the subject. You put the phone down.

Next time, you get through to the contact, but he's not authorised to talk to the media unless you go through the press office first. By now, you're desperate for a quote, but however hard you try, the only thing you can get him to say that would be even remotely quotable before he puts you through is, "It's a very interesting subject and there's a lot to say about it." He puts you through.

The entire press office is in a meeting. You get to leave a voicemail.

The next contact picks up his own phone but he can't fit you in until a ten-minute slot on Thursday afternoon. You do, however, manage to get him to tell you that (let's say), "The current regulatory position is very challenging, but I'm confident the industry can find a way through." You got him to say that by coming out with some phrase about this being a "challenging time", which is why you're doing the story. You make a note to ask a question about regulation. You hadn't known there was an issue there.

You're about to go back to your familiar list of contacts you always use. But now your luck changes. Now it starts to be done well.

You try one more number.

Your contact picks up the phone. You explain who you are and what you're researching.

"Okay. Fire away."

You ask your first question. Your contact answers it.

The answer is short, snappy, quotable and ends with, "Of course, you need to factor in the regulatory position, and I'd certainly want to think about the cost implications."

"So tell me about the regulatory position?" you say. You circle this name on your list, write "Ask about cost" on your notepad and underline it. Yes, the recorder is working.

That's one big fat quote sorted out, but you still need a few more. You try another number.

It's the switchboard, but they put you straight through. Next, the press office puts you straight through. So does the PA who comes on next.

Then you're put through to the office of somebody who's away until next week. But the voice that answered the phone says, "I can try to answer your questions if you like? I'm the technical manager. I work with him on this." You ask the questions and get the answers, and better still, this guy has an even wackier job title. Nobody else has ever quoted this guy!

You've got everything you need, but as you put the phone down, you realise that there is one more question you could ask.

You've got one more number to try. This time, the contact is away addressing a conference in Frankfurt on a subject that is just one click away from the subject you're researching. Would you like a transcript of the conference address? And although he won't have time to do an interview, would you like his email address so that you can send him any questions and he can email answers between conference sessions?

Oh yes.

How it's done badly by invitation

You're a journalist and invited to a one-to-one briefing over coffee in the contact's office. You arrive pretty much on time and you're told that the contact's previous meeting is running over. The only thing to read in the reception area is a rival title (or, if you're a TV journalist, let's say that the television is tuned to a rival channel). This is normal (see the next section).

After ten minutes, you see a journalist who works for a rival title being ushered out by an obvious PR, who returns to the lift without looking in your direction.

Five minutes after that, the same PR comes down and collects you. In the lift, he asks about the weather outside, says something about being cooped up all day, and then asks whether you've met the contact before. No.

"Oh, I think you'll like him. He's a very interesting man. I think you'll be very interested by what he has to say. It's a very good story."

You know very well that this is the launch of (let's say) a mutual fund investing in European smaller companies. And there have been several of those recently. The real question is whether this one gets one inch down the back of the news round-up or two inches up front. The very real question is whether this contact is going to come across as somebody who would be worth interviewing in the future. Do you keep his direct-line number, or do you throw away the whole press pack after you've written up the news item?

But you nod and say, "Sounds very interesting."

You're ushered into a small conference room. There's a press pack on your side of the table. A lot of papers strewn about on his side. Empty coffee cups.

He comes forward and thrusts a business card into your free hand. The PR does the introductions. He gets you more or less right, and you almost enjoy the bit where he goes on about what an authority you are. The contact has had a lot of job titles in his recent career. Most of them include at least one comma.

The PR is clearing away the coffee cups. This makes it impossible for them not to offer you a coffee. The contact won't, he's just had one, but do go ahead.

There's a hiatus while the PR calls out for another jug of coffee, which clearly hasn't been agreed in advance with catering. And he doesn't have the authority just to ring up and ask like this. (The coffee will arrive as you leave.)

The contact sits down facing you and talks for a while about how very pleased he is to be doing the job he's doing now, how excited he is by the new product, how very happy he is to have this chance to meet his friends in the media. While he's doing this, you're reading the papers he's got spread out in front of him. You've become very good at reading upside-down over the years.

One sheet is the day's agenda: you see that another of your rivals is getting the lunch while you're only getting coffee. Another is a memo giving circulation figures for your title and all the others he'll be meeting during the day. And – bingo! – there's also the sheet of sample answers to likely questions.

The contact gets to the end of his introductory blah and says something about giving you an opportunity to ask any questions you might have about the product.

You realise that he's brought you all the way here, and now he's expecting you to do the talking. You haven't prepared any questions, because he's supposed to be briefing you. So you ask the question you've just read off his briefing paper.

Luckily, it's one of the difficult ones.

"Journalists never forgive and never forget"

Remarks like this tend to be made by PR people who know how wide the gulf of understanding can be between their clients and the journalists who interview them.

They are not true: journalists interview so many people that they forget very easily (being remembered is the challenge) and they tend to be far too busy to waste mind space on forgiving or not forgiving.

The point of such remarks is to get across the point, as forcefully as possible, that the dishevelled youngster facing you across the desk has a very narrowly defined set of needs coupled with a very low tolerance for extraneous facts, and little time. If a journalist is going to remember anything beyond his current deadline, it's going to be the people who were really helpful, and the people who weren't.

What do we know so far?

If you're new to this, or if you're wondering why you never get calls from the media, here are some suggestions:

- **How easily can they get through to you?** All the expensive media training in the world won't help if the person who answers your phone won't put the call straight through. It really is very easy, actually. And if this is going to work well at all, you really are going to have to prepare yourself to receive unexpected calls from journalists needing a quick comment at short notice. Whether or not you're doing it deliberately, don't hide yourself away too effectively.

- **Journalists don't necessarily know the questions to ask.** If you don't know the answers, how are you going to know the questions? We'll get into this in more detail later in the book, but feel free to keep an interview going with suggestions of your own.

- **How much preparation do you need?** People do ask for questions in advance, and journalists do send them. But it's a bore, frankly. Are there questions you're afraid to be asked? Have you got something to hide? Can you and your people really not get what you need from the initial phone call?

- **PR people are wonderful, but don't let them get bureaucratic on you.** The point of a press office is to get media coverage, not to distribute memos about the number of times journalists have tried to get through to you. If you can't talk to journalists unless they go through the press office first, you won't be talking to many journalists.

- **Are you really the only person in your organisation who can talk to the media about your subject?** Are you serious? You mean, the entire organisation but for you is staffed by people who aren't competent to talk about what they do?

- Very few journalists are looking for in-depth, boffin-level, expert stuff. But **they'll work very hard to get you to say something quotable**.

- **If you don't give a journalist anything, you won't be quoted.** The fact that you're addressing a conference/on holiday/out to lunch won't persuade them to hold tomorrow morning's newspaper until you get back.

- That thing about the rival publication in reception? It's important, particularly if you deal with the trade press. It is unlikely that you will be in the habit of putting the trade papers out in reception for customers, et cetera, to read. But it is likely that trade journalists will be turning up every now and then to hear about your latest product. If you want them to like you, **do something more subtly flattering than telling them how important they are**.

- **Journalists can read upside down.**

- Journalists are human.

You're very interesting

This is worth a section of its own. It applies particularly if you're using public relations (see below), but it's also worth bearing in mind in any situation where an intermediary has put you into contact with the media.

When a journalist calls, or turns up to interview you, there's a good chance that she will have been told that (a) you're interesting, (b) you have something interesting to say and (c) that you're going to say it in an interesting way.

You will have been "sold" to the journalist as a potentially useful new contact. Your PR people (or other intermediary) will have succeeded in presenting you as likely to be more interesting than the people already in her contact book.

Live up to this.

Read yourself in

It makes a lot of sense to read at least something by the journalist who is coming to interview you.

Does this person, for example, use short quotes to start long paragraphs of explanation in her own voice that probably also came from the people she interviewed? Should you be coming up with short statements of the obvious points, or does she like long, more complicated quotes?

How many people did she interview for the piece you're reading? Frankly, do you get a sense that she does or doesn't know what she's talking about? She may not be writing about your subject on this occasion, but you can assume that she'll apply roughly similar amounts of research to every subject, and arrive at a roughly similar level of understanding.

If you're going on television or radio, watch/listen to an edition of the programme. How do they use their interviewees? How simplistic is the treatment of the subject? How long a sound bite does each interviewee get to deliver? If the programme doesn't have time for lengthy explanations, there's no point in saying anything complex enough to need explaining.

It is also prudent to check what you, or anybody else in your organisation, might have said in press releases or articles recently.

Oh, and by the way, if you're being interviewed by one magazine and another one rings up immediately afterwards, take both opportunities.

Now you've hit the middle-sized time, look after the juniors

If you're new to this, you'll be surprised at how quickly you become a "key player" or an "important figure" or even a "well-respected authority" or whatever phrase the journalist likes. You'll probably be dealing with the trade press, and they talk themselves up by talking up the people to whom they have access.

In terms of preparing for the media, the point is that you should always deal with the trade press as though you're dealing with the nationals. This is not just because it gives you a chance to practice your media-handling skills. There are two other reasons:

1   The nationals read the trades. Sometimes, they commission trade journalists. Often, they're called up by trade journalists offering freelance work.

2   Junior journalists grow up to be senior journalists.

One senior journalist on the financial pages of a national newspaper tells the story of her first-ever interview. Fresh out of journalism school, in the first week of her first job on an obscure little financial magazine, she was sent to interview a fund manager about his award-winning fund. After a couple of questions, the fund manager said, "You don't know anything about this, do you?" The journalist admitted that she didn't even know what a fund was. "Okay. Stop the tape." The fund manager came round to her side of the desk and gave her a ten-minute lesson on the very, very basics of fund management. Then he suggested a couple of good questions she could ask. Then he went back round to his side of the table and the interview re-started.

They're still friends.

In-house and external PR agencies

We'll start by defining terms. Then we'll talk about the role of PR, then we'll get onto what kind of PR you might find useful, and then, in the next section, we'll talk about paying for it.

For the purposes of this book, public relations is an activity whose sole purpose is handling contacts with the media. It is not corporate communications, although it may be close. It's not marketing, although it may be close. It's not advertising, although it may be close. And it is absolutely nothing to do with sales. Some PRs talk about "selling" a story into the media. But that is a very different kind of persuasion from your basic sales pitch. (Some companies hire PR people to keep them out of the media. We'll assume that you do want coverage.)

But that's enough definition. First, it is not true to say that you must approach the media via PR. You can do it yourself. The difference is that a PR person will be doing the job all the time. The PR person might get wind of stories in your field before you do, because the PR will be looking out for them, and it will be part of the PR person's job to know the right journalists to approach with whatever story you have.

> Note: An effective PR will be as closely tuned to what the media need, as to what you want to provide. In a working relationship with an effective PR, you should expect to spend at least as much time listening as talking.

The role of PR is to generate, first, column inches, and secondly, more importantly, ongoing relationships with key journalists and titles. We'll talk more about relationships in Chapter 2; for now, suffice to say that raising your media/public profile means more than just getting mentioned once or twice in the trade press. You might find that a "beauty contest" between PR agencies vying for your business degenerates into a series of flipchart/PowerPoint presentations on your brand positioning, with attendant technicalities, but don't get bogged down. There are three qualities that an effective PR person will need:

- **Chemistry**. Would you buy a used client from this person?

- **Enthusiasm**. Is this person interested enough to present you effectively?

- **Surprise**. Are there any ideas here that might lift you above the competition?

There's no science to PR, or if there is, it's second to a range of human qualities that frankly, you should like.

In slightly more detail, the role of PR is, first, to generate media-oriented paperwork and ideas for media-oriented paperwork. There are press releases to write and distribute, for example, and surveys to conduct, and whatever other initiatives might be, er, cooked up to generate media attention. There are likely interview questions to rehearse. After that, your PR person will arrange meetings with journalists, host meetings with journalists, and arrange any follow-up. Above all, PR people should know all the right journalists and know when to keep quiet.

If you're ever interrupted by a PR person while talking to a journalist, fire him (unless, of course, you were about to be embarrassingly indiscreet). If you're on a conference call with a journalist and a PR person, and all you can hear is the PR person breathing in the background, consider his position for him.

The role of PR agencies is not to understand the complexities of your business, beyond the point at which they become capable of writing your press releases, and nor is it to bring your message to the world. Nobody quotes PR people. They connect you to the journalists who can quote you, and if they're any good, they pressure you into producing what those journalists want.

One CEO, ousted after a buy-out of his company and speaking off the record about his future plans, said this of his former PR adviser. "I liked him. He was a one-man-band and we ran him off his feet sometimes, but he was always enthusiastic. I had the feeling he wanted it to work. I'll certainly use him again." PR people like to be told they're creative. A lot of them like to look busy, with mobiles always ringing, taxis always waiting. What matters is the chemistry. If they're any good, they want it to work.

You may already have an in-house PR function, or there may already be somebody in corporate communications/marketing who takes the media calls. Fine. You may want to find out what currently happens when somebody calls the switchboard and asks for the press office, but whatever it is, if it works, think about not fixing it. There is no substitute for anything that bridges the gap between the journalist's phone and the one you've got on your desk.

But if you're not that lucky already, you've got the choice between an internal restructuring and hiring an external agency (there are times when in-house and external PR might work well in combination). It may be that there's a budget for hiring an in-house PR person, or it may be that you prefer the arm's length, less committed relationship you can have with an agency. Either way, you need to take on somebody with authority, who can be independent.

If your PR does not have the clout, and indeed the knowledge of the business, to be able to pull either you or another appropriate spokesperson out of a meeting when the *Today* programme calls, you're wasting your money. (One sign of a good PR is that they make friends with the support staff who might one day have to do the actual pulling out.) Similarly, if your PR doesn't have the independence/authority to tell board members when their clever ideas for getting coverage are rubbish, you'll be paying good money to pitch ideas into editorial waste-paper baskets.

> *A variant on this problem occurs in firms where, for example, there might be value in putting the star fund managers, or the star litigators, or the leading authorities, or the key players, or whoever, in front of the media. The PR might be able to generate the interest and might take calls from journalists wanting interviews. But if nobody in the company buys into the idea that the PR guy's calls are worth returning, the whole idea is going to nosedive. You don't have to put your PR executive on the board, but before you start promising the big interviews, think this one through.*

An in-house PR executive (or department) will be likely to know more about your business than an outsider, but you might want to balance this against the likelihood that an external agency, with a range of clients and thus a wider range of opportunities for maintaining contacts with journalists, might be likely to know more about what those journalists actually want. You might also want to think about whether you'd be better suited by a large agency, where you might be dwarfed by other clients but where everybody would be more or less constantly in contact with the media, or by a one-man-and-his-work-experience-person outfit, where at least you will have the undivided attention of the chief executive at all times.

In-house marketing and PR departments are the first to be cut in times of economic slowdown. Then they're the first to be needed again when the recovery comes. This might be an argument for hiring an external agency that can be switched on and off as market conditions (and contract terms) dictate. It is also a factor to be taken into account when pondering the question of whether to take on full-time PR, or to hire an agency on an ad-hoc or project basis.

And then there's cost.

Paying for PR

If you call a business PR agency and ask what they charge, the chances are that you will find yourself discussing the length of a piece of string. However, there are some standards, and a commonly quoted figure for an annual retainer is £25–30,000pa, with costs on top for special projects such as product launches, annual results, et cetera. It is possible to pay significantly more than that, just as it is rumoured to be possible to negotiate your way down to the lower end of four figures with a small agency. "Sources close to the industry" (see the section on going off the record in Chapter 4) suggest that hiring a PR who has just left a big agency to set up on his own gives you big-agency contacts with small-agency enthusiasm.

Freebies, jollies, lunches, cuddly toys and contact numbers

What many journalists seem to like best is catching up with colleagues in circumstances where they don't have to take notes or look interested. If you're giving a media party at which all the journalists are talking to each other, believe me, it's going well. You don't have to butt in.

If you're giving a late-evening party, by the way, you'll make a better impression by providing taxis for the late-stayers at the end than by interrupting conversations to hand out your business card.

Lunch is a useful tool. Use it to get to know a journalist, or to reward a journalist who quotes you (but don't put it like that), or to remind a journalist who never quotes you that you exist, or just to get some time out from the office with somebody who isn't one of your colleagues. The need to get closer to a journalist can be a convincing reason to spend some budget on trying out a new restaurant, but don't be surprised if your guest was there last week with somebody else. When entertaining journalists, remember that everybody else does it too.

If you entertain customers and/or suppliers, you might like to try something similar with journalists. If so, it is probably wise not to combine customers and journalists, although there may be a case for hosting a media event jointly with one or more business partners. At a large-scale event, it makes a lot of sense to include one or two PR people in the party, to deal with such exceptions as, for example, the journalist who forgot his passport and will need to be put on a later flight.

If you are travelling with a large group of journalists, give some thought to the free time. Some of them might just want to go shopping after the lunch that follows the guided tour round, let's say, your new Paris office or your new development on the Costa, but others might welcome more structured entertainment. Don't just dump them all off on a sightseeing bus while you get down to some serious work. They'll know what you're doing.

Some journalists make a not-very-serious distinction between a "freebie" and a "jolly". A freebie will tend to have some vaguely work-related purpose. You could probably hand out a press release or introduce a new colleague. A jolly will tend not to be like that. Sometimes, freebies turn out half-way through to be jollies after all. It's rarely the other way round.

Whatever kind of trip you're planning, if you're distributing anything, either give it out at the end or include a bag. If you're into gifts, they will certainly use the pen, might use the diary and possibly even the mouse mat, but they probably won't thank you for another paperweight.

We are *not* talking about advertising here

There are some media outlets where you can buy influence by buying advertising. Some of them might be places where it's worth being seen. But as a general rule, seeking to influence a journalist by talking about your advertising spend will be counter-productive.

Most, if not all, journalists like to believe that they are hired to express an objective view of their subject. The word "objective" is probably worth a book in its own right, and we could fill up some space debating whether journalists are as well-informed and intelligent as some of them seem to think they are. But the general rule is:

approach any contact with the media on the basis that it is up to the journalist to decide how to use your contribution.

And finally ... the media-friendly enterprise

The media-friendly enterprise is full of people who pick up their own phones, return missed calls within the hour, and even when they're picking up somebody else's phone, offer at least to say something quotable if there isn't time for the right person to be found. In the media-friendly enterprise, PAs, receptionists, PR people and other support staff have the clout to call key spokespeople out of meetings for media calls, and nobody in the enterprise is ever criticised for what they're quoted as saying. If there's any internal tension or politics, it doesn't show.

The media-friendly enterprise doesn't exist. Yet.

2

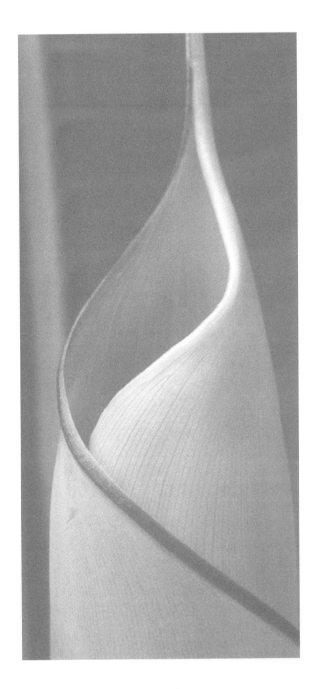

What Journalists Want,
And Why They Want It

Introduction

This chapter starts by looking at what journalists want at the most basic professional level, and then builds up to defining a more precise set of requirements that you might want to take into account when preparing for media contact. Chapter 3 then follows through by suggesting a number of techniques that you can use to prepare your own story, whatever it might be, so that it will be most effective at interview.

The intention of this chapter is *not* to suggest that you should set aside what you want to say, and instead start looking for something that will suit the journalist who is coming to interview you. No. The idea is that, once you know what a journalist is looking for, you can present your story in such a way that it both meets all the journalist's expectations of what a good story should be, and also gets across what you want to say.

There is one fundamental point from which everything else flows. It is this:

> Journalists are in business to sell newspapers and magazines. Or attract larger audiences to radio and television programmes. Everything else is secondary to this. If a journalist's output doesn't persuade people to turn the page, or tune in to the programme again next week, that journalist has failed.

This is not to say that finding things out, getting the facts right, quoting you accurately, et cetera, are not important, but that all of those concerns are secondary to the commercial objective. They matter, because there's no market for inaccuracy (in a business context, at least), but if the newspapers remain stacked in the warehouse, or the radio/TV is not switched on for the programme, the whole effort has been wasted.

In practice, this means that a journalist will approach an interview thinking one thing above all else:

> How can I use this to create something that will hold the attention of my audience?

Sometimes, the answer may be that a straightforward accounting of the facts will be enough. But if you spend some time retrospectively analysing the features in a newspaper that caught your attention, you may conclude that there's more to it than that.

You may also notice that although most business people carry briefcases-full of papers giving straightforward accounts of facts that matter to them, they still buy newspapers and magazines.

There are times when it's right to spend your morning train ride flicking through the previous quarter's sales figures, and there are times when the figures can wait because you feel like reading more of your newspaper than (say) just the news in brief and the market report. Part of the attraction of the media is that newspapers, et cetera, do provide you with information that you need. Part of it is also the range of techniques that a title uses to convince you that you need it more than perhaps you really do. These include everything from marketing and advertising down to the size of the headlines and the serious expressions on the presenters' faces.

Individual stories, by individual journalists, will also seek to convince you, first, that you're reading something that matters, and secondly, that the experience of reading it is either rewarding, or enjoyable, or both. This doesn't work all the time. But any story in the media says more than just, "Here are the facts." It also finds ways to say (or imply), "These facts matter," and indeed, "You need to know these facts right now."

Over time, you may also come to feel that you have a relationship with your regular newspaper, or with one or more of its writers/columnists. You don't.

Here's the point:

> When you're interviewed, the journalist will be thinking at least as much about how well your words will fit into a persuasive package, as about the truth (or importance) of what you're saying.

In the media, presentation matters. It matters because you need to be convinced that you're reading something that's worthwhile. What journalists want is the raw material to enable them to produce eye-catching, readable, up-to-the-minute, "important" or even "major" stories that will add value to their audience's day. When a journalist turns up to interview you, therefore, he's thinking about presentation as well as content. The aim of this chapter is to persuade you to do the same. We'll work through the basics, through what journalists want, and then we'll get into presenting what you want to say.

Covered in this chapter:

- A brief word about the word "story"

- The basics 1: who's the audience?

- The basics 2: what's the news?

- The basics 3: where's the skill in this?

- Beyond the basics: journalists want to fill empty space

- Journalists want to fill empty space in time for their deadline

- Journalists want to fill empty space in a way that impresses their editor and persuades their audience to come back for more

- What do you have, that might interest a journalist?

- What can you provide, that the journalist can't get without you?

- Journalists want it now

- Journalists want relationships with reliable contacts

- And finally … the media-friendly contact that all journalists want

A brief word about the word "story"

Almost all journalists use the word "story" to describe whatever item of content they're preparing. They may use other words as well – feature, article, package – but the bottom line is that they're really setting out to tell you a story.

Whether you associate the word "story" with children's stories, or with something else, it is useful to think of journalism as a form of storytelling rather than, as it were, a form of "fact-retelling". Note also that when one journalist wants to know what another is working on, the question will almost certainly *not* be, "What's your subject?" but rather, "What's your story?"

More about this later.

The basics 1: who's the audience?

There are two audiences. The first is the large group of disparate strangers who buy the title (or tune in, et cetera). Their characteristics and requirements are defined for the journalist by a range of inputs. First, there's the title itself. You can work out who reads *Professional Nurse*, for example, or indeed *Swimming Magazine*. You can pretty much guess what they want to read in their magazine. Then there's market research. And feedback such as readers' letters. And increasingly, there's experience. The journalist gets to know readers, advertisers and other interested parties. Perhaps the journalist was recruited for his nursing experience or his enthusiasm for swimming.

The second audience is The Editor. The journalist needs to produce stories that convey such messages as: I know what I'm talking about; I have done some research; I have good contacts in the industry; I deserve a pay rise and/or promotion. The Editor will be busier than the journalist, dealing with all the stories coming in, and he will tend to know less about the subject of any individual story than the journalist who wrote it. But The Editor will know a good story when he sees one.

Don't overlook that second audience. What's needed to placate The Editor may be, for example, a regular flow of exclusive news stories that no rival journalist has got, or good ideas for future stories. It may simply be a matter of quoting a minimum of three people in every story, to prove that the research has been done. But one thing is certain, as they say on television: if you can help a journalist provide for his second audience as well as his first, you'll be popular.

More on this later, as well.

The basics 2: what's the news?

You know it already of course, but if you deal regularly with journalists, you will become even more familiar with the word "news". This is a term that needs definition. The "news" is not just what's read off the autocue by a newscaster every evening. It's what will interest the audience of the specific title in question. There's a selection process involved: it's all news, but what's a headline, what's a short filler item? The "news" is also the plural of the "new", as in new information or new story.

So far, so obvious. What's important here is that nine out of ten journalists prefer their news to be surprising, quirky, unpredictable, different, eye-catching. A "news story" will not necessarily be complete, therefore, just because it contains an item of new information. There may be some presentation work to be done on it as well, perhaps emphasising the surprising detail, writing an eye-catching headline.

This has practical implications. One perfectly good answer to this chapter's title question would be: journalists want news. They probably also want it simple, and quick, and exclusive. It's probably worth adding that if they come to your office, or indeed anywhere else at your invitation during their working hours, they want it big enough to justify the time spent away from the office.

That's it. Almost.

Suppose your news is the release of your end-of-year results. If so, it will only really be a news story if you have dramatically exceeded/failed to meet expectations, or if your new biotech division has under/outperformed by a large margin. Perhaps your industrial-chemicals division has emitted no carbon whatsoever this year; perhaps whole cities are gasping for breath.

Your results will be news but not a news story if everybody turned up for work, everything went well, and you turned in a performance that surprises nobody.

Remember the selection process: where's the detail in your news that gives you front-page coverage rather than a column inch at the back?

Now read on.

The basics 3: where's the skill in this?

As suggested in this chapter's introduction, journalists need to do more than just present the facts as you provide them in your interview. Their job is to produce a story that might ideally be well-informed, timely and authoritative, but that absolutely must be eye-catching, thought-provoking and entertaining. Not only that, but it must be capable of appealing to the widest possible audience.

Then they have to do it again. And again. And again. The complicating factor is that every time they prepare a story, it's got to be the same as last time, but different. You know what you expect from a story in the *Financial Times*, for example. But you don't actually want the same story every day. It's got to be an FT story every day, but each time it's got to be a different FT story.

The professional skill of the journalist, therefore, lies as much in fitting the facts of a series of different subjects into a series of similar stories, as it does in working out what to write in any particular story. In practice, therefore, the skill is to gather just the amount of information necessary to write a readable story in the appropriate house style, and then to forget the lot and get on with researching and writing something else in the same house style.

Note that sequence: research it, write it, forget it; research it, write it, forget it; research it, write it, forget it; do it again. Also work out the speed at which the cycle spins. The frequency of publication of a given title is also the frequency at which its journalists have to forget what they've just been doing and start again with a blank sheet of paper or a blank screen.

Let's look at that in more depth.

Beyond the basics: journalists want to fill empty space

This applies to all journalists, all the time. Whether the space happens to be a two-minute gap between the big political interview and the sports news on tomorrow's morning radio show, or three pages of next week's issue of a mass-circulation magazine with the words 'Cover Story' printed at the top of each page, or a single column inch at the back end of next Sunday's Business Section's news round-up, the real task, the one that really matters, is to fill it.

Happily, journalists get what they want. Somehow, there's always enough news to fill the scheduled length of every news broadcast, just as somehow, there are always enough celebrities in love triangles to fill the gossip magazines and just enough chief executives denying rumours of a bid approach to fill the business pages. After all, when did you last hear a newsreader tell you that it's a quiet night, nothing much happening, so they're packing up early?

Your favourite voice on the radio might switch from an in-depth, no-holds-barred interview with a government minister about the imminent collapse of civilisation to a two-minute piece on how to make your window-boxes hedgehog-friendly, but at least there hasn't been any silence.

Here's a useful definition:

A story is something that will fill a gap.

And here's a question:

   Is a story something that is important or interesting?

Answer:

   Not necessarily.

With some exceptions (deaths of prominent people, massive corporate bankruptcies, et cetera) the first test of a story is whether there's a space to fill. If there's no space, your story would have to be very important and very interesting to be included in the issue. But if there's a very large gap and nothing else to fill it, your story could be just about anything and still get taken up. This is where the journalist would start working to make even your most insignificant little story sound more important than it is.

There's no standard applied to whether a story is big enough or important enough to be included in a title. If there's space, and it would work as a space-filler, you're in. So don't waste time wondering about whether a journalist will consider your contribution newsworthy.

Journalists want to fill empty space in time for their deadline

This is obvious, but it's often overlooked. The Sunday papers don't get held over to Monday because there's a gap and they want to find something interesting to fill it. Newspapers go out every day and magazines every week or month, while, the radio keeps on talking and the twenty-four-hour rolling news channels keep on rolling.

If you still think journalists are primarily motivated by a mission to explain, or an urge to bring you the world's top stories as they happen, or a philanthropic desire to equip you to succeed in today's competitive marketplace, spend a minute in a newsagent. Perhaps flick through a TV/radio listings magazine. Think of all that white space and silence that will have to be filled before the next issues of all these newspapers and magazines, the next episodes of all these programmes, are due to come out. Journalists fill empty space, and as a rule, they do it in a hurry.

Think about the journalist whose job it is to fill, say, the news pages at the front end of the trade magazine you flick through every Friday lunchtime. This individual is probably also writing one of the features, finding pictures for the whole issue and, let's say, editing the letters page. She's got until 5pm tonight to plug a three-inch gap on the last news page and she's run out of press releases.

If you called her now, how dramatic and interesting would your news have to be, to be taken down and used in that three-inch gap? If you offered her a picture or a chart to go with the story, would you have a chance of getting shunted to the top of that news page? (See Chapter 6 for good times and bad times to call journalists.)

If you called her late tomorrow or the next day, after this issue but before she's even started to think about next week's news stories, do you think she'd be just as interested? Or not.

You don't have to be interesting to get news coverage. You just have to be interesting enough. At the last minute before a deadline strikes, that may not be very interesting at all.

But you can't be late.

Journalists don't wait.

There's more.

Journalists want to fill empty space in a way that impresses their editor and persuades their audience to come back for more

This section is not intended to contradict the preceding two sections. Filling space on time is important. Sometimes, every journalist has to resort to space-fillers, and every title almost certainly contains a few items that got in because there was still space to fill at the last moment. But you can't take the same approach throughout.

Filling space on time is easy compared to filling it interestingly. If a deadline is fast approaching, there will (almost) always be somebody who calls, a press release to copy out, or an obliging contact to ring up for a snappy(ish) one-liner, or a single-issue enthusiast burning to be interviewed about (say) hedgehogs and window-boxes. And there will always be room, at some point in the production schedule, for that kind of space-filler.

But most of any regular publication or broadcast programme has to deliver, or look as though it's delivering, what its title promises it will deliver. If it doesn't, it dies. This is basic commercial common sense, as true for the *Financial Times*, *Management Today*, *Gardens Illustrated* and *Machine Knitting Monthly*, for example, as it is for *Airline Business*, *Commercial Motor*, *Music Week*, *Conference & Incentive Travel Magazine* and *Packaging News*. On the air, the same goes for, say, *The Today Programme*, *The Money Programme*, *In Business*, *You & Yours*, *Newsnight*, *Today's Business* and *Poetry Please*.

And if the title doesn't say it all, the promotional literature will. *Management Today*, for example, is "an award-winning, informed, frank and challenging monthly business magazine". Its articles give "practical advice to help managers at all levels to advance their careers and develop their business". CNBC Europe's *Today's Business* programme is not only a "fast-paced, one-hour, one-stop-shop," but it also "provides everything you need to know before you head off to work in the morning". And they do it every day. Sixty minutes of "everything you need to know" before you've even finished your power breakfast. And they don't even know you.

That is a very tough challenge for the collection of typically young-ish media types whose job it is to turn this stuff out day after day.

Think of all those editors and producers, constantly looking for something that will put their title ahead of the competition. Think of all those "Exclusive!" tags you see on newspapers, for example. Think of how many times you've heard the phrase "Only in the *Sun/Mirror/Daily Mail* tomorrow!" This is a competitive business.

Think of all those editors. They're busier than the journalists and know less about the subject of each new story than the journalist who wrote it. But they know a good story when they see one. It will have an attention-grabbing first line and they won't have to skim through it more than once to get what it's about.

And then think of all those journalists trying to give their editors what they want. It's true that journalists want to fill empty space, and to do so on time. But what they really want is to convince their editors that they are delivering interesting informative, entertaining content that can't be found elsewhere. They want to impress the editor that they know what they're talking about and do their research, and they want their readers (listeners, viewers) to come back for more.

Crucially, because their editors are so busy, et cetera, they're concerned to make their stories *look* well-researched and informative. The story has to look good as well as (ideally) be good.

So what does this tell us?

- Journalists do want to fill empty space. They do want to do it in time for their deadlines. If you time your approach right, there's a chance they'll take just about anything vaguely relevant from you.

- But what journalists really want is something interesting, informative, competitive, et cetera, that will make them look good.

- If they can't get anything interesting, they will want something that can be made to look interesting.

- Whatever they get, interesting or not, they will be concerned to make it look as interesting, up-to-the-minute and informative as possible.

Give them what they want often enough, and they'll write you up regularly and remember you fondly while they're doing it.

This leads us to an obvious problem:

> In real life, nothing's really that interesting.

The journalist is interviewing you because he's doing a story, not because he's interested. He's writing it for an audience that needs to be convinced. Even if he is thinking, "Wow! This is really interesting!" he's also got to think, "How can I make it obvious that this is so interesting?"

If nothing is intrinsically interesting, he's got to apply a set of techniques to make it seem interesting.

This is where you come in.

What do you have, that might interest a journalist?

Given that we're still talking about what you can deliver in the course of an interview, there are two possible answers to this question:

1   Stories.

2   Components of stories, like quotes, et cetera.

We'll start with the notion of your giving a journalist a story that he didn't have already. Hold the thought that underneath it all, journalists are not motivated by an intense interest in you and your company, but by a need to fill space competitively.

Think first about what these people don't want. They don't want a cover story from you every month. Nor do they want a call from you every week at the same time with yet another idea. They don't want predictability. They don't want the next issue to remind everybody of the previous issue.

They want variety, unpredictability, interest. They want originality. They want items of different lengths, colourful pages (or screens), new people, new ideas. They want to surprise the audience. Within the confines of the overall brief (*Management Today* has to be about management; *Investors Chronicle* has to be a chronicle for investors) they want to be different every time. Whether they're preparing the feature pages, the news, the diary, the two-minute item before the sports news, the market round-up, they want something that's new.

But the interview has already started and it's a fair bet that the journalist has already got a story in mind. No problem. Your advantage is this:

You know all the **angles**.

A really competitive story will have at least one really competitive angle. The best definition of an angle might be that it's the story within the story, or perhaps better, that it's the fastest, most attention-grabbing version of the story. The *subject* is a big, static thing (your line of business) while the *story* gets it moving (something's happening in your line of business) and the *angle* gets it moving faster and adds a few hairpin bends (while that's happening, there's also a giant ape climbing up the outside of your office building).

Back in the real world, suppose that the subject of the story is, let's say, domestic insurance. And the story is that premiums are rising because of a recent steep increase in the number of burglary claims. Because you're in the business, you know all the angles. The journalist might have latched on to the angle that, let's say, although the number of claims has risen, their overall value has stayed more or less the same. Therefore, he wants to write, the premium increases may not be justified.

That's fine as an angle, and it will make up most of the story. But imagine how much better his story would be, if you let him in on the angle that the reason for the premium increases is not the burglary claims, although they're a factor, but a policy decision that low-value clients are bad business because they don't take enough security precautions. Better, eh?

Here's your opportunity:

> A journalist will always be on the lookout for a better angle.

A really competitive angle is unique. It says: you won't get this elsewhere.

An angle also gives a story the opportunity to develop. You might hear a news report that, say, the stock market has crashed. The immediate angle is all those billions knocked off share prices. Then the angle shifts and multiplies. Traders are facing job losses. Pension funds can't meet their capital-adequacy margins. A day-trading grandmother put her life savings into the market half an hour before it crashed. Were investors wrongly advised to get into the market? Prices are going up again, but will the recovery hold? As the sun goes down on a bad day for the market, one thing is certain: it's the same subject – the crash – but the angles just go on multiplying. (Where are prices on the anniversary of the crash? Has that grandmother been compensated by her adviser?)

In that kind of story, a good angle will challenge the consensus. If you come out with the view that the crash is good news (low prices, opportunities) while everybody else is still moaning about how bad it is, they'll send a limousine to get you to the studio. But remember: timing. Once everybody else has twigged the low-prices angle, you'll need something else.

If you want to give a journalist a story, you have to come up with a more competitive angle than he has already. "The market crash" is a subject. "Prices falling faster than ever before" is a story. But it's the story that everybody's got. "The market's crashing and prices are falling but my hedge fund is making millions and I know somebody whose Tarot cards told him to get out yesterday" is a subject and a story and a couple of angles.

The journalist has the subject, and probably a story with a reasonable angle. But you know all the angles, and it's probable that you could suggest a better angle for the story, or even a whole better story based on what you know and he doesn't.

Before you interrupt a journalist with your idea of what he should be asking you about, read Chapter 4 on handling the interview. Before you do that, consider these characteristics of a story. If you're going to suggest something, here's what it should look like:

- A story will be **narrower than its subject**. It may focus in on only one aspect, or angle, within an overall subject. In a business story, there will be facts and figures (if at all possible). Readers want facts, but more important than that, journalists like to give the impression that they know what they're talking about. There will probably also be charts, graphs and photographs. They look good, and sometimes, they're even useful. You could provide those.

- A story will be **visual**. The man on the Clapham omnibus, the veteran hack in the crumpled trench coat, the teacher with chalk-stained fingers and the single mum on a tight budget would all prefer to read about one in three people than about thirty per cent of the population. Make it real. Use examples. And if you can possibly come up with a case study of a real-live customer, I want it.

- A story will have a **human-interest element**. See above. But also think about the reader. How is the story going to affect the investor reading *Investors Chronicle*, for example?

So far, despite everything we've said about you knowing all the angles, all of the above could be found and knocked into a story without reference to you or anyone like you. There are press releases to be copied out or rewritten, for example, and there's the internet. But there's one component of a story that a journalist can't find alone.

What can you provide, that the journalist can't get without you?

A story will contain **quotes**. Journalists can't quote themselves. Quotes, or sound bites, give authority to a story. They prove that the journalist has done some research, that the publication, or programme, is well-informed by virtue of having sources to quote, and that, frankly, this isn't just some space-filling waffle thrown together at the last minute by some two-bit hack.

Quotes tend to be short, pithy and, whenever possible, vividly expressed and eye-catching. Policies differ as to how many quotes a story should contain, although a print-based freelance writing a story for the feature pages of a magazine might aim for a minimum of three, but "more than one in most cases" would be a useful rule of thumb.

When you're thinking about being quoted, divide journalists into two groups. There are those who think they know their subject and have a fair number of established contacts lined up to provide quotes, and there are those who are, to put it politely, a little hazy about the finer details of whatever it is they're supposed to be writing about. The first group can't go through their professional lives only ever quoting the same little group of people. The second group is in great need of people who can explain, in quotable English, what they should be saying.

For both groups, you need to make it easy. The know-it-alls are likely to be impatient with a potential new contact who doesn't come straight out with something quotable, while the second group needs to be thinking, simultaneously, "I can quote this person!" and "I can understand this person!" within minutes of your coming on the phone.

You will have things you want to be quoted saying by journalists, and we will come onto the task of preparing what you want to say in a quotable (understandable) way in Chapter 3. For now, here are the key features of a good quote:

- A good quote will pass the **opposites test**.

  This is because a good quote actually says something. If you tell a journalist, "We look after our customers," don't expect to be quoted. You would never say the opposite, "We neglect our customers," so you're not really saying anything. But if you tell a journalist, "We invest our clients' money to achieve capital growth," you might claim to invest for income, which is more or less the opposite strategy, so you have imparted quotable information.

- Two other tests can be applied to a quote.

- The first is the **common-sense test**. "All of our customer-service operatives are tirelessly dedicated to our customers' welfare." Gimme a break. On Friday evening? All of them? With a claim like that, it's wise to have an example ready. Even wiser to leave the example to speak for itself. "Here's an example of the kind of customer care we can provide. At 6am on the morning of her wedding day, Julie here got a call from a customer with a flat tyre ..."

- The other test is the "So what?' test". Try and say something memorable, please. Don't just toe the party line.

And if you're worried about the internal audience, your boss, his boss and everybody else in the company, the strategy you need to adopt is:

Forget them.

And if you can't do that, focus on building up a media profile over time (see below). You do know what you're talking about. You have got something to say. Keep saying it. And remember, if you run into an internal-politics issue, you're the one with the cuttings file tucked away next to your CV. You can always murmur something about being misquoted. Nobody trusts journalists anyway.

Journalists want it now

Journalists focus on the end product. If they are print journalists, they are most concerned to produce a news story, or a feature, or a diary item, or whatever else, on deadline. If they're broadcast journalists, they will be concerned to produce an end product that sounds (and looks) right on deadline. Time, particularly in broadcast journalism, is neither elastic nor negotiable.

What this means is that journalists are not attracted to process. If you work for an organisation that has meetings, whether they're board meetings, team meetings, staff meetings, production meetings, marketing meetings, even crisis meetings, you might have to adjust your mindset if you're going to deal effectively with journalists.

Why? Because of the process. In any organisation, any meeting will tend to involve a setting-up process. Where the meeting is important, the setting-up process will tend to include a period during which PAs talk to PAs, diaries are got together, emails are exchanged, timings are confirmed. Then there will be agendas to draw up and circulate, other papers to get together, reading to do in advance, meeting rooms to be booked, coffee to be arranged, caterers to be placated. The more important a meeting is, the more likely it is that there will be a pre-meeting process to go through before it can happen (and a post-meeting process afterwards).

If you've got a meeting scheduled with a journalist at which you're going to be interviewed, that isn't how you handle it. Cut the process. Same goes for telephone interviews: cut out as much of the setting-up process as you can. Journalists don't like process.

Why?

- Because a journalist will want to connect to you, do the interview, disconnect and go away again. Nothing else. No memos, no confirmation, nothing.

Why?

- Because the interview is not the end product. It's only one of the components that has to be collected together and assembled into the end product.

Suppose you're an expert on dogs. You're recording an interview with a TV reporter for a local-news item on how, let's say, dogs make perfect pets for children who aren't doing so well at school. Your interview is very important, of course, but what's actually filling the journalist's mind is that the piece won't work at all unless she can find a puppy and a small child who are willing to be filmed together. She wants to use that piece of film for her voice-over intro.

If you happened to have a six-year-old daughter with a puppy, you'd be very popular. But the emails confirming the time of the interview, the follow-up call asking her if she wants anything else – she's busy phoning round the local kennels and vets, actually. Kindly get off the phone.

Best advice for when you're being interviewed?

Just do it.

Journalists want relationships with reliable contacts

Journalists want sources, contacts and relationships with sources and contacts. Ringing up a total stranger is a high-risk business for a journalist. The total stranger may not talk to the media, or may refer the call to the PR department, or may come on the line and say nothing, at length. Even worse, the total stranger may be only too keen to talk to the media, but impenetrably and without saying anything quotable. Most journalists dislike having to admit their own ignorance, unless it's to somebody they know well.

So journalists tend to ring up the same people, over and over again. They ring the people who will almost certainly be available, who will answer their own phones, and who will produce quotable answers on demand. Such people will tend to have good pictures of themselves readily available. They will *never* say, "The answers to all these questions are in the press pack I sent you three months ago."

It is a very good thing to build up relationships with key journalists in your field. This does not mean bombarding them with invitations to go out clubbing just as their deadline hits. It does mean being available, speaking clear, quotable English, reading the stuff they write, taking them out to lunch occasionally, giving them stuff that nobody else has got. Journalists don't need personal friends in your line of business, but they do need the contact details of people who will make their job easier.

The other thing about building up relationships with journalists is that they'll be that much more willing to return your calls. After all, if you've got an idea for a story, it's easier to try it out on somebody you know.

And of course, there's crisis management. We'll come to that in detail later (Chapter 7), but for now, suffice to say that in a crisis, you need people around who'll listen to your side of the story.

And finally … the media-friendly contact that all journalists want

The media-friendly contact that all journalists want is a person who always answers the phone, always has something to say, and always says it in neat, vivid sentences that are easy to cut out and quote. The media-friendly contact never assumes that you'll remember what was said last time you called for an interview, and never minds if, this time, you don't quote anything but just use it all for background. The media-friendly contact never puts you on speakerphone and never asks to approve quotes.

The media-friendly contact doesn't exist … yet.

3

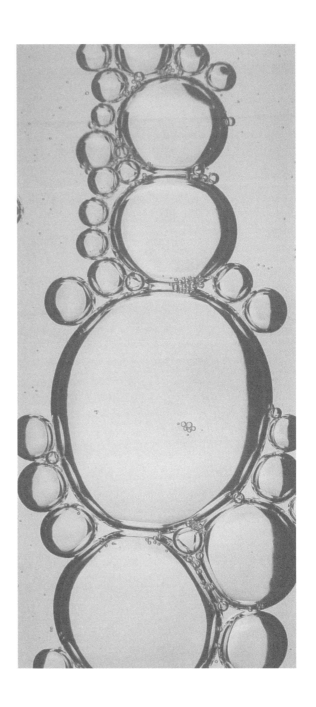

Getting Your Message Straight

Introduction

To start with a definition:

Your message is the single thing you most want to get across in an interview.

It's also the impression you want to give. If the journalist is going to quote only one of the things you say, this is the one you want quoted. It's related to the subject of the interview and it's a demonstration of your insightfulness, wisdom, et cetera. Note the word "demonstration" there. You can't just say you're clever; you have to show it.

To take that a step further:

Your message is what you want to transmit through the journalist to the audience beyond.

It's the impression you most want the reader, listener, viewer to get of you, your company, your product. Note that a message can be more than just a single quotable statement. Having a message can mean going into an interview with an objective in mind such as, "I want to get across that we focus on getting every detail right." Or it can mean going in with three sentences that you'd like to deliver as quotes.

When we talk about your message, we might be talking about three bullet points that you can jot down on an index card and take into the interview, as above, or we might not. We might just be talking about an impression. But the real difficulty with this chapter is that we have to switch direction half-way through. It is a very good idea to work out the message you want to convey to the media, both generally and in the context of whatever specific interview you might have coming up. But once you've done that, it is also a very good idea to put your message aside and be as spontaneous, lively, pro-active as you can in the interview itself. Because that's a message in itself.

This is, therefore, a chapter about getting yourself focused and ready for contact with the media. It's about interview preparation.

> *Working out your message is a process that lies somewhere between deciding who you are, in the sense of how you want to be presented by the media, and deciding what you want to say. It's the ten minutes you spend with a notepad and perhaps a couple of colleagues, thinking through the subject of the coming interview. It's even a step towards controlling the interview, in that going in knowing that you're (say) a dynamic executive with a lot to say about the subject beats sitting back and waiting for the first question.*

Given that the next chapter is called "Handling the interview", this one could as easily be called "Handling the pre-interview".

So why isn't it called that? Because there's a distinct value in identifying and projecting a message, however amorphous that message might be. Your message is not exactly your brand, nor is it quite your image, but it is consistent with both of those and supports them.

But why do we need to talk about messages, when we've already talked about quotes? Three reasons:

1   The strength of a message transmitted through the media (excluding advertising, of course) is that it comes with the implicit third-party endorsement of the journalist and the title in question. There's already a message in the fact that you're the authority being quoted, but you want the whole portrayal of you to be favourable.

2   A message can affect what the journalist thinks. Being known to provide good quotes is positive. But if a journalist "gets the message" about you, that can affect what's written in the paragraphs around your quote.

3   With a clear message to convey, you're using the interview rather than being used for the interview.

Your message can just be something you say. If you want the world to know that you've just upgraded all your computer systems, for example, say so, and then line up something else to say about the upgrade's functionality, and then mention something that you couldn't do before and a lot of people still can't do.

But remember that your message can also be more all-embracing and more subliminal than just a set of quotes. If the journalist goes away thinking, "Wow! He knows what he's talking about," you've got a worthwhile message across. When you say something quotable, you're delivering a component of the journalist's story. But when you think about your message, you're thinking about your own game plan for the interview.

Now read on.

Covered in this chapter:

- Getting the endorsement of the title

- Brainstorming your message

- Your story v. their story

- Self-belief is a message

- Beyond brainstorming

- Falling back into the old trap

- Finding the elusive message

- Handling the off-message interview

- And finally … what makes a good message?

Getting the endorsement of the title

As suggested above, your presence in a journalist's story conveys the implicit message that you are an authority on the subject under examination. In effect, that adds up to an unspoken endorsement of you and your company. It will not be necessary to put the words "As seen on television!" on your business card, because anybody who saw you will already have the sense that the TV company has pinpointed you as the voice of authority on your subject. This is not necessarily a very big thing, but it's there.

Journalists working for serious titles don't just give that kind of endorsement away. Nor do they retain whatever credibility they have with their audience by just providing a platform for corporate self-promotion. Journalists have to convey at least the impression of editorial independence, and at a very pragmatic level, they can't plug one company for fear of annoying all the others.

As the previous chapter made clear, any title's most important relationship is its relationship with its readers. There is a trust issue here. Even if you're an advertiser – especially if you're an advertiser – you can't be seen to enjoy a special relationship.

> *There are grey areas, but if you're new to this, you'll be a lot more successful with journalists in the long term if you don't start by throwing your advertising budget around. And remember that you wouldn't be advertising if the title couldn't attract an audience that you can't otherwise reach.*

So your message has to take a form that the title can endorse. Remember that you already have the implicit endorsement of the title by being featured. Now consider this proposition:

> The value of media coverage is directly proportional to the audience's acceptance that the impressions given and opinions expressed in a story are the title's and not yours.

You might have a lot of clout with a small trade title, and that might be obvious to everybody, but your customers will be more impressed if you say something that gets quoted by a major newspaper where you have no clout whatsoever.

> *Note: Strictly speaking, whether this is made explicit or not, a title is not endorsing you because it mentions you and/or quotes you; it certainly does not endorse the views expressed in your quotes. We're talking about audience impressions here, rather than legal niceties.*

So here, once again, is rule one:

1   Don't sell.

   This isn't your interview. It's the journalist's. She's not offering you a space to talk about yourself.

   And anyway, you won't be quoted if you just extol your own virtues.

Here's rule two:

2   In the context of getting your message straight, don't even think about selling.

As we shall see in the next section, it is important that your message should take into account the subject under discussion in the interview. Start from that rather than trying to find a way of projecting your company that isn't selling but that has the effect of selling. A coherent message clearly expressed will sell perfectly effectively without any help from you.

Now read on.

Brainstorming your message

You know what the interview's going to be about. You've asked as many questions as you can in advance, and you know that the journalist wants to ask you questions about, say, investment with particular emphasis on emerging markets.

Probably the most useful thing you could do now is sit down with a pad of paper and perhaps a couple of colleagues, and work out what you want to say.

But don't start by looking for a message in the space between emerging markets and your company. Look outwards. Because here's the punch-line to the whole chapter:

You already know the questions you're going to be asked.

Think about it. You're being interviewed on investment with particular emphasis on emerging markets. Unless the journalist has made an unusual mistake, this is because you're somebody who knows a bit about investment, and there's something in the public domain that suggests you know about emerging markets. (If you're a divorce lawyer in Hull, with no knowledge of investment whatsoever, cancel the interview now.)

Don't start by brainstorming your message. Unless you joined the company yesterday, you'll come to that quickly enough. Start by brainstorming the questions any sane and reasonably well-informed journalist would be likely to ask you now. What actually is happening in emerging markets at the moment? Have any markets emerged and are any new ones emerging? What about Latin America? Is there anything to be said about trading fiddly little emerging-market currencies?

And so on. Because the opportunity here is not that the journalist doesn't yet know the answers to the big questions. The opportunity is this:

The journalist doesn't know the questions.

This time last week, the journalist was researching something completely different. How on earth should she know what to ask you about your specialist subject?

An effective structure for your brainstorming session might be, first, to establish what issues are likely to arise in an interview with a journalist who's been given a brief, who's then spent some time on the net, plus some time reading cuttings and past notes, and who might already have interviewed a couple of other people (she might also have written about emerging markets before, but months ago). Then work out what questions the journalist should be asking, if she was as well-informed as you are.

From this process, you will get a fairly comprehensive template for the interview. Use this as the basis from which to work out your most effective message(s). Staying with the investment/emerging market example, you might decide that emerging markets are excessively volatile at the moment. If your company markets highly diversified, play-it-safe unit trusts, you'll want to get in something about diversification as a way of reducing the risk of volatile markets. But if you're targeting high-net-worth sophisticated investors, you might decide to talk about market timing, volatility as a potential source of high performance, et cetera.

You go into the interview keen to talk about diversification/volatility. That's your message, and it addresses whatever questions the journalist has prepared. You don't sell anything and you don't even mention your company. Result: the journalist quotes you first and files away your contact details for the future. And funnily enough, if anybody in the audience is looking for a company that's good on diversification/volatility, they come to you.

It is a common mistake to believe that a media interview is a form of interrogation (or discussion) in which one side knows the questions and the other side knows the answers. Actually, in most real-life media interviews, one side knows both the right questions to ask and the answers, while the other side is pretty good at listening and picking up references to things that matter.

There's a caveat to this. The journalist might not know the questions, but she might not realise that she doesn't know the questions. Her preliminary research might have given her a clear, but out-of-date and probably inaccurate, idea of the questions she should ask. This potential problem is addressed in the next section, and then we'll move on to discuss good and not-so-good messages, and their application.

Your story v. their story

Any journalist will almost certainly turn up to an interview with an idea of what you're going to say, plus a list of questions to get the thing started. This doesn't mean that the journalist has done a lot of research, or indeed knows what she's talking about. Unless the journalist's questions all focus on a particular angle, in which case she's decided what she's going to write about, you are free to assume that your idea of what issues are important is as good as hers. After all, it is likely that you do know what you're talking about. If you didn't, she wouldn't be here.

You don't refuse to ask a stupid question. Nor do you dictate the better questions. That would be very tactless. No. You steer the interview.

There are consecutive sections in Chapter 4 entitled "Control and direction" and "Leading answers and simple cues" respectively. They address this tactic in detail. Here, the points to be made are:

- Any alert journalist will be ready to be led in an interview.

- If you have a coherent message worked out, and it influences the answers you give, you will be leading the interview whether or not you realise what you're doing.

If the interview is about emerging markets and your whole message is about caution, you will not have any trouble leading from the question, "Are you optimistic about the prospects for emerging markets?" Cautiously, yes. But there are some risks of which the investor should be aware. "What are those risks?" And off you go.

And if your whole message is about opportunities for sophisticated investors? Yes, you're optimistic. In fact, there are exciting opportunities to be found. "What are those opportunities?" And off you go.

These are narrow examples, but the principle is, if you have a clear idea of the message you want to put across, you're in a stronger position than the journalist, whose clearest idea is just that she wants to get you talking.

More on this in Chapter 4. Now let's put together your message.

Self-belief is a message

Here's a quick point to make before we go any further. Always go into an interview looking confident and enthusiastic. If you're reluctant, or uneasy for any reason, this will transmit. Always be pleased to see journalists. Or be good at pretending.

Beyond brainstorming

Do not necessarily adjust your message in accordance with this section. However, do consider whether your message lends itself to effective delivery.

You have brainstormed the subject of your interview and come up with, say, three bullet points expressing a theme that you'd like to convey. Now there's the question of how you deliver that message. This is partly a matter of body language and partly a matter of sincerity, as above, but there's also the point that if you can't actually deliver your message as though you mean it, you've failed.

There is a section in Chapter 4 entitled "Attitude and delivery". Briefly, its message is that you should behave in an interview as though you believe in what you're saying, which of course you do, and as though you're enthusiastic about what you're saying, which of course you are. But before you even get to the interview, think about the extent to which your message affects your delivery.

If you're not going to be able to say it while meeting the journalist's eye and sitting forward in your chair, think about that. Elsewhere in this book, you will find the point made that you should tell the truth in an interview, even if the truth is inconvenient (and especially in a crisis). You are unlikely to come up with a message that is a lie, but it is just about possible that you might come up with a message that does not express your personal conviction.

There are a couple of reasons why this might happen. The first is that you're in the wrong job. Frankly, that's your problem. But the second reason is potentially more useful. There is a category of message that works perfectly well in a brainstorming session, but that doesn't stand up in the light of day.

Remember the audience. They're discussed at greater length in Chapter 2 and elsewhere in this book, but in message terms, the point is that they're unlikely to be tuning in to the media with the same quality of attention that they give to, say, technical reports or company briefings. They're in sandwich-eating or going-home-on-the-train mode.

Therefore, your message will be most effective if it is personal, or at least person-to-person rather than, say, corporate-to-counterparty. If there are compelling reasons why you have to deliver a message that is politically correct in company terms (see the next section), think privately about whether you can find a message within the message that is personal, or whether you can move on from the corporate part to something that will be more useful to the journalist.

Falling back into the old trap

It is very easy to fall into the trap of trying to manipulate an interview back towards a point at which you can deliver a promotional statement about your company. You're prepared to go along with all this stuff about messages and quotes, but you know that what you're really going to do, as soon as the opportunity arises, is alert the journalist to the fact that she's talking to a director of a company that's much better than its competitors, has the best products known to man, and deserves to be upgraded from the short piece she's doing for the business pages, to a front-page splash with accompanying free corporate brochure.

You may even believe all that. There are also situations where you have to say it. The chairman and the chief executive might have decided to sit in on the interview, disguised as filing cabinets, and it might be time for your annual performance review. There might be rumours of redundancies.

If possible, don't do the promotional bit first. Certainly, don't make it the whole of the interview. Why not?

Because it won't get used.

You'll find this point made several times during the course of this book. Why is it being made again here? Because of what happens in real life and in media training.

Handling the media gets easier with experience. For this reason, a lot of any media-training session is taken up with role-played interviews. The trainees practice everything from a chat with a trade journalist to a full-blown studio-based TV interview. Sometimes, they even get to review the day's papers on morning television.

You might (not) be surprised at the number of trainees who want to start role-played interviews on tightly defined topics with ten minutes on how their company was founded a long time ago, looks after its customers, cares, has good products, et cetera. All wonderful, but all totally unusable and frankly annoying. It happens in real life too. But it's worse in media training because people do it within minutes of being told not to do it. And it's training, so they could pretend. But don't.

The practical point here is, frankly: beware of your default waffle. It's easy to talk about what you know, in the corporate sense, and you can even kid yourself that because you're talking, you're giving an interview. But you're not. You're talking your way out of the journalist's contact book.

Finding the elusive message

So far, we've talked about brainstorming a message and making it personal. We've talked about how the possession of a clear message enables you to lead an interview, and we've discussed the potential trap of doing everything right and then delivering an impersonal non-message anyway.

We've also considered the point that a message is at its most deliverable when it expresses a personal conviction. So let's pick up that point and examine one potential source of an effective and deliverable message that is often overlooked: your opinions.

It may be that your personal opinions on your industry are at least as good a source of interview material as the in-house corporate stuff you're immersed in every day. This is not to suggest that you should make yourself into some kind of loose cannon, but it is likely that if you had to keep a conversation going about your industry at a trade function or even a social event, you could come up with some opinions. Not to make too much of this point, but those are at least some of the interesting things about your industry. They're also the things you know more about than anybody else.

If you can, get those out into the open. Here's why:

When you're dealing with the media, it's good to be opinionated.

Not all of your opinions will be appropriate to bring out in an interview of course. If you said what you really think about everything, you'd probably become an ex-director very quickly. Fair enough. The point here is to invite you to think about how you look, sound and feel when you're expressing a strongly held opinion. If you work for a life company, you might have strong opinions on unit-linked policies. Ditto if you're in the food business and keen to argue for butter as a much-under-rated health food. Let's assume you hold either or both of those two beliefs. If they came up in an interview, or in any reasonably serious conversation, how would you handle it?

You'd want to be heard and you'd want to be understood. You'd think about what you were going to say and how you were going to say it. You'd do whatever it is you do to get everybody's attention. Then you might, for example, lean forward over your desk and explain your views very clearly and simply, possibly even enumerating points on your fingers. You'd be alert to whether people were nodding, wanting to ask questions, wanting to move on because they'd got it. But however you did it, your approach would be very clearly directed to getting the other person really to understand and become convinced by what you were saying.

Great. Fantastic. Hold that pose.

The combination of strongly held view and commitment to expressing it clearly?

That's a message.

At the end of an interview that has gone perfectly, the journalist will return to her office convinced that, say, unit-linked investment is a good thing, and/or that people should eat more butter. She believes it, so her whole story will express that view. She'll not only quote you as an authority to back up her case, but the whole story will convey the message that you've given her. Doesn't happen often, but it's good when it does.

Handling the off-message interview

As suggested earlier, having a message can be just knowing that you'd like to get something across. If this is an interview about investment, let's say, and you're a director of a unit-trust company, you might go into the studio hoping to say something about the importance of diversifying an investment portfolio across a range of assets, and if possible also about investor education, and if possible also about customer service (but see below). If you can speak on any one of those subjects, you will connect your company in the audience's mind with the idea of diversification, education, service.

And that's the message you want to get across. So you walk into the interview with "diversification, education, service" in the back of your mind. And you remember that you can only get your message across indirectly. If the audience thinks, "Aha! This guy is trying to promote his diversified fund," you have worse than halved any positive impact the interview might have. An interview should feel like a conversation between informed observers of its subject, rather than self-interested participants, and in any case, you want to be invited back.

Fine.

But you encounter a problem:

You don't get an opportunity to deliver your message.

Staying with the example above, the journalist might want to focus on the prospects for emerging markets, so you never get a chance to say a word about diversification, et cetera.

You have a couple of options, all of which are positive. The first is:

- **Go with the flow**. Any single interview is best treated as part of a longer relationship. If the journalist gets more out of this one than you do, that's fine. Remember that just by showing up, you gain the implicit endorsement of the title, which has a vested interest in presenting you as an expert (and thus vindication of their superior expert-finding skills).

- **Rethink your message**. Of course, it's a little late to do this once you're in the interview, but if the journalist is asking about emerging markets, you might switch easily enough from, say, "To invest successfully, diversify," to, let's say, "Emerging markets are best treated as part of a diversified portfolio." A good message is flexible.

- **Wait**. If the journalist is any good, she'll finish by asking whether you want to add anything else. There's a whole section in Chapter 4 about when not to take up this invitation, but if you've still got stuff to say, say it. You can always say, "Can I just add one more thing?" if you don't get asked.

It's a good thing to have a message that you want to get across in an interview. But don't try too hard. There's already a message in the fact that you're the expert being interviewed. There would be a negative message in being detected trying to sell. In this business, there's more to lose by trying too hard, than there is by sitting back and relaxing.

> *About customer service. It's a big issue nowadays. But it's potentially negative. If you mention it, assume that the journalist will be on the line to your call centre/helpline immediately after the interview.*

And finally ... what makes a good message?

Your message is your own, but here's a brief summary of what looks and sounds good from the other side of the microphone:

- Opinions

- Assertions

- Arguments

- Strongly held views

- Controversial views

- Strongly held beliefs of all kinds

- Specific examples

- Pictorial language

Enough. You get the idea. Of those eight, take the first six and use the last two to express them. You will be quoted.

While we're at it, what doesn't make a good message?

- The company line

- The status quo

- Generalisations

- Platitudes

- Statements of the obvious

- You are so predictable

- You would say that, wouldn't you?

- Everybody would say that, wouldn't they?

- Erm, er, you see, er, um, er ...

See? It's easy.

Now we've got all that straight, Chapter 4 will take you through the interview itself.

4

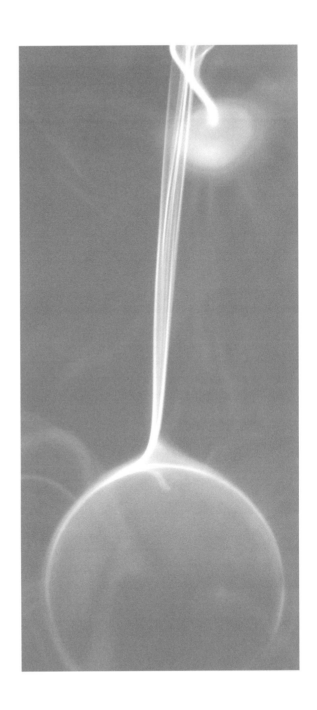

Handling The Interview

Introduction

This is a chapter about coming face-to-face with journalists who want to take down everything you say and use it to entertain and/or inform their public. We'll start with the face-to-face, one-to-one interview, and then move on to discuss the press conference and finally the television interview. Along the way, we'll take in the various other possible encounters with journalists, from straightforward telephone interviews through lunches and social events to radio phone-ins involving members of the public.

Covered in this chapter:

- All media contact starts when it starts

- Questions you should ask

- Media policies are only as good as the people who ignore them

- Going off the record

- Recording devices

- Attitude and delivery

- Control and direction

- Leading answers and simple cues

- Dirty tricks and devious cunning

- Hostile questions and challenging interviews

- Silence

- Why?

- The totally idiotic follow-up question

- The stunningly ignorant question

- Horizontal ignorance

- The technology breaks down

- Telephone calls

- The role of PR in an interview

- Interviews in person

- One-to-one briefings over coffee and an agenda

- Lunch

- Press conferences

- Round-table discussions, wine-tastings and other gimmickry

- Dealing with members of the public

- And finally … all media contact ends when it ends

All media contact starts when it starts

The first and probably most important point to make is that **the interview starts at the first contact with the journalist**. Not when you're both sat down with coffee and biscuits and you've said your little bit about how you're always happy to help your friends in the media. You're about half-way through by then.

So start by thinking about your office and your people. Whatever your line of business, whatever message you want to get across to the media, you probably also want to project the impression that you represent an efficient, well-run organisation, and that you yourself are a popular member of a happy band of workers servicing a happy band of customers.

You will not project this impression if, for example, the print journalist turns up at your offices to find that the only reading matter in reception is a rival publication. Nor will it work particularly well if the receptionist is not briefed in advance. "There's somebody here to see Brian. Says she's a journalist." Invest five minutes in making sure that the trip from the front door to your office is a happy one and a quick one.

Do the same with the phone system and your diary. When you're dealing with the media, effectiveness is answering the phone. If the call has to be routed through six people and ten minutes of hold music, you'll be lucky if there's anybody still waiting by the time you get on the line. And it's fine to tell your staff that you alone can talk to the media, but make sure they understand that they can disclose, for example, your mobile number or the useful information that you're due back in ten minutes. Make sure that you get messages quickly.

If you're really keen to talk to the media, and especially if you're the only person in your entire organisation who's able to discuss your subject, make sure junior staff understand that they can pull you out of meetings if a journalist calls.

Here are some facts:

- In many companies, even the most junior staff are authorised to interrupt director-level meetings if a media campaign is under way and they take a call from a journalist.

- A lot of people do hand out their direct-line, mobile and home phone numbers to journalists.

- Talking to the media is a competitive business. If a journalist can't talk to you, she'll talk to the next person on her list. Chances are, that person will be a competitor.

It may or may not be a fundamental rule of business that you should get on well with the people between you and the outside world, but it's always kind of obvious if your secretary, the people on reception and the people around the office like you enough to go the extra mile if there's a screw-up with the interview arrangements (as, surprisingly often, there is).

If they don't care enough to help, and the FT journalist ends up ringing you on her mobile from reception to find out if you know she's there, you can be sure you're going to read about it in the profile she's researching.

And for goodness' sake, look around you. There's a City firm that spent a day briefing journalists on a new product launch. It was only when they read four out of nine of the resulting news write-ups, that they found out about the consignment of toilet rolls that had spent all of that morning conspicuously stacked next to reception. Journalists always like to include something different.

Questions you should ask

If you are telephoning a journalist, for any reason other than returning a call, always ask:

- **Is this a good time to talk?** If it isn't, ask when would be a better time and **get off the phone**. The single most effective way of not getting coverage from a journalist, ever, is to say, "This won't take a minute," and then launch into your exciting piece of news just ten minutes before their deadline. They won't be listening. They probably won't even have the phone close to their ear. But they will remember that you're so stupid you don't even know about deadlines. More on bad times to call journalists in Chapter 6.

Most of the time, of course, you won't be making the call that initiates the interview. But there are still questions you might usefully ask. Generally, a good interview is one in which you do the talking and the journalist just slots in questions at regular intervals. But it helps to know that you're saying the right things rather than just wasting time. So before you start, try asking:

- **What do you need?** The answer, however it's expressed, can be taken to mean, "I'd like you to say quotable things about … " Especially if it's a big subject, you might want to break this down a bit. So try asking:

- **Is there any particular angle you want to take, or shall we just talk generally?** If what's required here is just a general chat, you might want to drop in the odd cue. The journalist might not know about the latest big development (because journalists tend to cover more than one subject and your industry doesn't come up that often), so you could ask:

- **Would you be interested in talking about [whatever is the latest big development]?** You can throw this one into the conversation before the interview. Another good reason to answer your own calls. You're the only one who can suggest all the subjects a journalist might like to talk about, that would suit you.

But by now, it's probably time to get on with the interview. Other questions you might want to ask at the beginning include:

- **Is this going out live?** If it's a broadcast interview, and it's not going out live, you can say "Er" whenever you feel like it, and re-start your answers as necessary.

- **How are you going to use this?** There can be times when it's useful to know that you're being interviewed for a long feature, for example, in which case you can drop in references to related subjects that (a) you know all about and (b) would work as separate boxed-text mini-features to break up the page. If you're being asked for a short space-filling one-liner (they may not put it like that), take it as a compliment and get your quote in early.

- **Can I see any quotes before you use them?** Please don't say this unless you really must, and if you do, please don't correct anything that isn't directly related to the meaning of what you said, or wish you'd said. Changing "while" to "whilst" throughout is just irritating.

- **When's your deadline?** Sometimes, it's worth asking this. You may have a relevant product launch coming up next week, for example.

Remember that journalists don't relax until they've got something quotable on tape. Asking a whole load of unnecessary questions is not, therefore, a good way of relaxing into an interview.

Good questions to ask towards the end might include:

- **Would you be interested in somebody who could tell you about ... ?** Check this in advance, but journalists like getting new contacts, and you might have business associates with relevant expertise who would appreciate being put forward.

- **Would you be interested in a case history?** Yes. If they're genuine members of the public with a genuine member-of-the-public story to tell.

- **Do you need pictures at all?** Yep.

- **I've got some useful charts, graphs and other page-decorating materials, if you're interested?** Yep.

And finally, here are a couple of things you would be well advised not to say.

- **This is all background, isn't it?** You're not going to quote anything I've said, are you?

- **That was all off the record, of course, wasn't it?**

If you agree to be interviewed, you run the risk of being quoted. On rare occasions, if it's agreed in advance, a journalist will interview you for background. But it's wise to follow the rule: if you're talking within earshot of a journalist, you might be quoted.

We'll discuss the whole "off the record" thing after a few words on the usefulness or otherwise of media policies.

Media policies are only as good as the people who ignore them

Your company might have a policy on dealing with the media. All enquiries should go through the PR department, for example. Only senior staff can talk to the media, and even they can only talk about their own area of expertise.

Such policies are no doubt very useful, and sometimes they're even necessary. You don't want junior staff making statements that might affect the share price, for example.

But build in some flexibility. If there's a journalist you've got to know quite well, who frequently writes stories in which you'd love to be quoted, don't oblige her to go through the PR department every time. If your media policy means you can't give out your direct-line number to people you want to call you, there's something wrong with it.

And if you've got a media policy that's designed to keep track of your company's contacts with the media, junk it. The bureaucrats might like to have a spreadsheet showing the number of times the media called, et cetera, but journalists just want to get quotes on tape. If they can't get you easily, they'll get somebody else.

Think about junior staff. They can't talk about company policy, of course, and you don't want them drawn into conversations where they end up letting slip some piece of information that can fill a gap in a story. But nor do you want them forbidden to talk to the media to the extent that they won't divulge when you're next available to take a call.

Brief them to help with the connection between you and the journalist. Equip them with airy phrases such as, "Oh you'll have to ask him/her about that." Remember the cautionary tale of the youngster who wouldn't even confirm the spelling of his line manager's name, so convinced was he that he shouldn't speak to the media.

Going off the record

Nothing's off the record. If there's something that you absolutely do not want to be quoted as saying, don't say it. If there's something that the journalist could usefully be told, but that you don't want to be quoted saying, spell it out in advance that you want to go off the record. Then take the risk. But remember that it is still a risk.

A lot of the time, going off the record works perfectly easily. But you have to say it in advance, and if you say something off the record that would make an absolutely one hundred per cent wonderful quote, don't be surprised if it gets quoted somehow. "A source close to the industry" or "an insider" or some other nebulous figure might say it, for example, or it might just be transcribed without quotation marks. The only snag with that is where you're the only person quoted nearby and it's the kind of thing you might have said. Journalists proverbially refuse to identify their sources, but that isn't much comfort if you're the only possible source.

Going off the record works most reliably where you know the journalist and you're likely to be useful again in future. Even then, if you're going to disclose something really sensitive, remember (a) that all journalists use recording devices, and (b) that chances are, there are people around you who know you're doing the interview.

Once you've said whatever it is, make it clear that you're quotable again. Sometimes, going off the record can be too successful.

Recording devices

There is a section on the legal questions that arise when an interview is recorded in Chapter 8. This section is about what happens in day-to-day life.

Everybody records everything. Journalists bring digital recorders to interviews, and you can judge how you're doing by how frequently they check that the machine is working. As to telephone interviews, you can buy little microphones that stick to the handset of a landline, or you can buy mobiles that record calls (sticking those microphones to mobiles doesn't work), or you can buy any number of desktop systems that plug into the phone socket or the PC and record everything that's said. While some recording devices bleep every five seconds to betray their own presence, others are silent. Try entering "recording device" or "phone recorder" into Google.

Recording interviews is taken for granted and not generally disclosed in advance. You might want to remember this:

> You can't always tell when a microphone or camera is live. Little red lights can be covered up. Sneaky journalists sometimes just "forget" to turn their technology off.

Apart from that, there's not a lot to be said about recording devices. Everybody uses them, everybody takes them for granted, a lot of words get recorded and some of them get played back. Many journalists record their interviews because they can't take notes fast enough. Their recording devices have counters, and when you say something quotable, they just write down the number on the counter rather than what you said.

You might wonder whether any journalist ever plays back the whole of a taped interview. You might ask yourself whether it would be wise to get your important quotes in early, before the journalist gets bored and misses bits while listening to the highlights. You might be right to worry.

Attitude and delivery

First, **attitude**. You know what you're talking about, right? You're being interviewed, so the logic of the situation is that **you're an authority on your own subject**. That's the part you play in an interview.

You're **interested** in your subject, and not only that, you're **enthusiastic** about it. You want to share your enthusiasm and get across what it is about the subject that interests you. You're also **serious** about it. Not serious in the sense that you can't smile, but serious in the sense that the subject matters.

This is not the party where somebody says, "What do you do?" and goes to sleep half-way through your answer. This is an interview with somebody who is being paid good money (a) to research your subject and (b) to take you seriously as a speaker on your subject. If the interview has been set up by a PR agency, the PR person will have "sold" you to the journalist as **knowledgeable, interesting, quotable and talkative** on the subject. So that's who you are.

Here are two important points:

1   **Your subject is interesting.** There may be people in the world who think your subject is boring, but they don't include the journalist, who's being paid to be interested, and they don't include the journalist's audience, who want to read/hear/watch what you have to say about it.

2   **Your job is interesting.** If it isn't, act as though it is. Watching people talking about a job they like, or a subject that interests them, is good television regardless of what the job/subject is. If you really don't like your job, maybe you shouldn't be doing it. But that's another book.

If you actually do enjoy talking about your job, or your subject, you're lucky. If not, talk about your job/subject as though the journalist is being paid to listen to you talk about, let's say, your recent holiday in Mauritius, or your child's recent success in the Grade 4 piano exam, or the train set you're building in the attic, or the curtains you've chosen to go with the carpet in the main bedroom.

Remember to stop regularly and wait for the next question.

Delivery. Because you are so interested, interesting, enthusiastic, et cetera, you don't sit well back in your chair, all bunched up, speaking in a monotone. You don't hang one arm over the back of your chair (subconsciously climbing over the furniture to get away from the journalist is a sign of unease; don't do it half-way through, either). But nor do you lean right forward into the journalist's face, using your arms like windmills and talking so enthusiastically that the journalist can't get a question in edgeways.

The idea is to express yourself. Not to over-express or under-express yourself.

So the obvious piece of advice is: be yourself.

Another possibly useful piece of advice is to speak to the journalist as though you're speaking to a friend before the interview, who's just asked you, "What are you going to say in the interview?" Aim for that relaxed account of what you want to say.

By the way, never answer that question. If a friend, colleague or partner asks you in advance what you're going to say in an interview, give a non-specific, vague answer. Don't rehearse your best quotes in advance. You need **spontaneity** in an interview.

Above all, relax or pretend to relax. Go into the interview assuming that you and the journalist share an interest in the subject and that both of you are enthusiastic about discussing it. This is almost certainly the truth of the matter.

The big mistake is to go into an interview expecting the journalist to ask difficult questions, or to be hostile, or to try to trip you up. In any normal interview, a journalist will start out neutral but anxious to get something quotable on tape. If you're defensive from the start and not saying anything worthwhile, the journalist's job becomes more difficult, so she might try asking questions designed to unsettle you, startle you, get you angry, or anything else just to get you to talk. She's still neutral, but now she's taking on the challenge of getting you to talk.

Here's some reassurance. Nobody believes it, but everybody finds it to be true.

> **Tough interviews are more successful than easy interviews**. There's something about adrenalin, or being challenged, or really having to insist on getting your point across, that makes an interview work really well for both parties. We're not talking about crisis management here (for that, see Chapter 7), but about your basic day-to-day interview between a journalist who needs something to quote and an interviewee who isn't coming up with the goods.

In an interview, you have something to say. You want people to share it, you're interested, enthusiastic, et cetera. So you're going to express yourself. You're going to talk, remembering to stop when the journalist shows signs of wanting to ask a question. You'll probably lean forward, because that's more positive than leaning back, and if it comes naturally, you might want to wave your hands around – but don't overdo it. Animation is good in moderation.

And if, at the end, you wonder how it went, there's a simple test. If an interview is successful, the chances are that you both enjoy it.

Control and direction

For a senior executive, this is often the difficult part. You spend your working life surrounded by people who do what you tell them. You're important. People listen to you, and act on what you say.

Now you've got to deal with a journalist. This person is not deferential in the subtle way that (maybe you hadn't realised until now) the people around you in the office are deferential. This person doesn't take dictation when you answer a question. This person doesn't seem to be impressed by your power, influence, job title, office size, obvious importance, whatever. You've got a busy schedule, but this person doesn't seem aware that you're doing her a favour by seeing her.

And this person just doesn't look like the kind of person with whom you usually have meetings.

If any of the above sounds at all familiar, consider this. You live your working life in a hierarchy. The journalist doesn't (not in the same way, anyway; see Chapter 2). And even if you're the chief executive, the very fact that the journalist is interviewing you means that she will have probably booked interviews with three other chief executives this week, and then maybe a couple more next week. If she's researching something that involves interviewing chief executives, and you're a chief executive, your role in her life is as one of the names on her list of possible interviewees. If she's found it easy to get access to you, you've gone into a database of chief executives she might call next time.

The key point is: no journalist researches anything by interviewing just one person. If she's interviewing you, it's likely she's interviewing other people like you in other companies. Everything cancels out, therefore, except how easy you are to interview.

There's more in Chapter 2 about the kind of people who become journalists, and what journalism does to them. Now let's talk about how you **control** an interview with a journalist.

First rule: don't try to get control. That isn't how you do it. However senior you are, and however junior-looking the journalist, don't try to "pull rank" if you ever want to be contacted again. (Probably best not to mention that you know the editor or the managing director, either. Junior journalists grow into senior journalists, moving from title to title, and have long memories.)

You control an interview by being useful. It is therefore more appropriate to think in terms of how you might **direct** an interview. This is done by subtle means.

First, you're accessible. You've recognised that a journalist represents a means of accessing thousands of potential customers and a lot of other people besides. You, your company and your brand will potentially be affected by the way this journalist retails the information you have given her, and the impression you have made on her.

So you have invested a disproportionate amount of management time in ensuring that this particular journalist has had an easy journey from first finding your name to getting into this interview. Don't do any kind of cost/benefit analysis here. Do focus on details.

If you're as good as you think you are, you're looking at/speaking to a happy journalist who's impressed with your company's efficiency. You've probably made sure the coffee's hot, too.

You might reflect on all the things you're doing that a chief executive doesn't do. You might wonder whether that sets you apart from all the other chief executives on the contact list. Interesting thought.

Now. Here's what you don't do:

- **Don't sell**. Not in any way whatsoever. You are not closing a deal, selling a product, pitching for a contract, whatever. Not least because the journalist is gathering information from others like you, her job is not to decide that you're best and write you up to the exclusion of all others. Her job is to find an angle on the subject of your interview, and write about it.

Here's why not:

- **You can't "win" an interview**. Journalists value their freedom to make up their own minds, which is what distinguishes them from just about everybody else, and if you waste interview time with a sales pitch, they will take this as, first, an insult to their intelligence, and secondly, an attempt to dictate their conclusions to them. They write for their readers, not for you. Their readers are not for sale; their readers are not buying.

This is fundamentally important. Remember also that a journalist's first duty is to her readers and second duty to the editor (or vice-versa), and that her career in journalism will be short if she gets into the habit of "puffing" her favourite contacts and writing stuff that sounds like brochure copy. She's got to sound independent, at least. (Okay, there are tiny little trade papers where journalistic independence doesn't really count for much, but even there, it's flattering to pretend, especially if you want to build up long-term relationships.)

Also, without contradicting anything said in Chapter 3 about getting your message clear and ready for delivery, the worst interviewees are those who come to the table with a rigid agenda that includes a spiel about how good their company is. (If you rubbish a rival, the journalist will interview the rival, just to see what happens. Every time.)

There's a kind of semi-rule that you might not want to break in the first five minutes, at least:

- Don't be first to mention your company name. The exception is where the journalist tries to warm you up by starting with the question, "Tell me about the company." Tell her, but don't go on for very long. She's not going to quote any of this stuff. Also, any answer beginning with the words "Here at Sales Pitch Limited, we … " is best avoided.

Here's what you do:

- You listen. And watch.

- You're flexible.

- You co-operate.

- You might even think in terms of humouring the journalist.

You need to "aim off" here. Favourable coverage, and a mutually beneficial long-term relationship with this journalist, is best approached as a by-product of a successful interview.

Really? Yes. It's a good thing, of course, to get your company name (spelled correctly) in print or on screen. If that's your objective, fine. But it is a better thing to give the journalist, and through her the public, the impression that you are approachable, expert, et cetera. This is because, let's face it, your casual reader isn't going to take in every word of a feature, any more than a TV viewer, say, will register every word of a news item. But what we all pick up, more or less instinctively, is an impression of whether we like the person being presented. That comes across in tone of voice, appearance, and in print, the write-up surrounding your quote.

What you want is a reader/viewer who thinks not only, "He sounds like he knows what he's talking about," but also, "I like the sound of him," and less consciously, "I could go to him if I had a problem with [your area of expertise]."

But you can't tell a journalist to write you up as though she likes you. Better just to get her on your side.

You can do two specific things to direct an interview: provide leading answers and hear simple cues, which are both discussed in detail in the next section. For now, let's just stay with the idea that you're dealing with somebody who:

- Doesn't know the subject half as well as you do;

- Doesn't know the right questions to ask, let alone the answers;

- Hasn't been keeping up with the key issues in your industry;

- Wasn't paying attention when something big happened last week;

- Doesn't want to be spoon-fed the substance of her story;

- Wants to find out but doesn't want to be told without asking;

- Probably doesn't want to admit ignorance; and

- Probably does want friends – contacts, at least – in the industry.

There's also a reasonable chance that your journalist is working off a brief written by somebody who knows less about the subject than she does.

> *Note: Journalists often conceal their knowledge. They can't quote themselves, so they ask questions to which they already know the answer, to get a quote. Sometimes, journalists knowingly ask stupid questions, just to find out what you say. Sometimes, they just ask stupid questions. Keep a straight face. This is not a waste of your time.*

So what do you do specifically? Here's a clue:

A journalist is always listening for the next question.

What do you mean, listening for the next question?

I mean that although journalists always turn up with questions prepared, they're actually listening to your answers for better questions.

Better in what sense?

Better in the sense that what you say is based on up-to-date knowledge of the industry. A good interviewee will say what he wants to say in short, quotable sentences. A good interviewee will be flexible. After what happened last week, a good interviewee will also listen.

What happened last week?

See what I mean? It's as simple as that. I've got the message across about listening and being flexible, and now I've directed the interview towards what happened last week.

Tell me more about listening.

Except that it hasn't worked. I want to tell you about last week, but you're asking about listening. Being a good listener, I'm going to forget last week (might try again later) and tell you this: if a journalist starts asking about a particular angle, or a particular detail, go along with it. You've got her interested, and if you're lucky, the thing you're dropping hints about is going to be her story. As the saying goes, it's not rocket science.

Rocket science? Where does that fit in?

Oops. Hold the thought that although you can't, and shouldn't try to, control an interview, you can direct it through what you say, and we'll move on to those leading answers and simple cues.

Leading answers and simple cues

Here's the thing. You go into an interview with a clear idea of what you want to say. That's based on your commercial objectives, of course, all mixed in with what the journalist claims to be interested in, plus what's been happening recently in your industry.

The journalist, who hasn't tuned in to your industry since about three features ago, turns up with a set of questions based on the brief for the feature, half an hour surfing the internet, and whatever she's learned from the interviews she's done already. She may have done some background reading on your company, but then again … she may not.

It may be that she's explicitly interested in hearing about everything that's been happening recently, or it may be that she's done enough research already to discover an angle for her feature.

Either way, she's alert to anything you might say that she hasn't picked up yet. The danger for journalists is failing to spot the thing that's so obvious that nobody bothers to mention it. Don't assume knowledge. Please.

> *By the way, there's almost always an opportunity to talk to a researcher before you do a TV/radio interview; they really do want to hear about all the current issues on which they could base questions.*

Here are two apparently contradictory pieces of advice:

1   Never assume, when a journalist asks a question, that the answer is the only thing she wants to know.

2   Never assume that a journalist wants to know more than she asks.

Any journalist will want you to provide quotable answers to her questions. But any journalist will also want to go back to the office equipped with the information to produce the right end-product. They don't want to go out with yesterday's big story.

So answer the questions. But feel free to steer the conversation via the odd hint that something else is important too. Don't just change the subject. Don't say, "Why aren't you asking me about … ?" But do equip yourself with little phrases like, "Of course, the other aspect of that is …," then say what it is, briefly, and shut up. If they're interested, they'll ask.

And if they do, go with the flow. You can think of this as providing them with cues. The other side of it is that if a journalist suddenly starts asking about one narrow little angle on your subject, whether or not you've led her to it, take the hint. It's your turn to pick up the cue. Once a journalist spots an angle that she likes, everything else becomes irrelevant. Even if you've got a wealth of information about something else, you probably won't get her away from it.

Let's go on to talk about a couple of things that can happen in an interview.

Dirty tricks and devious cunning

We might as well face it. What a journalist wants out of an interview and what you want out of an interview are two different things. We've talked about quotes, sound bites, messages, stories, et cetera, but what it all boils down to, at the very simplest level, is that a journalist will want you to talk and keep on talking.

This can't always be achieved by asking questions. Your first answer might be short, complete and devoid of anything that might suggest a follow-up question. Your second, third and fourth answers might be the same. If you're too controlled, a journalist might try some trickery to get you talking more freely.

If this starts happening, there's an important point to remember:

> If a journalist seems to be trying to trick you, or trip you up, or knock you off balance, the motive is almost always just to get you to talk more freely.

There are exceptions, of course. If you're a politician, or if your company is involved in a bid, or if your results are out soon, or if you're in mid-crisis (see Chapter 7), there may be other motives. But a point to remember is:

> If a journalist is seriously trying to get you to say something you don't want to say, chances are you won't be surprised. You probably know what it is, too. And you probably shouldn't be doing the interview.

Most of the time, frankly, journalists just want to get the job done. But as we've said, this means getting you to talk freely, and sometimes, getting you to talk freely means using a few tricks.

In the next sections, we'll discuss a few of them. There are others, and all journalists develop their own interview techniques, but these turn up frequently.

Hostile questions and challenging interviews

Most of what you need to know about handling hostile questions is covered in the previous section, above. Because it's a big issue, here are some further comments.

If the question is aimed at getting you to admit the truth, for example that you did lay off hundreds of employees five years ago, you have to say so. It may be that conditions have changed, that you contributed generously to retraining, et cetera, but your answer does, sooner rather than later, have to contain the word "Yes".

Once it does, you can move on. Unless you're being interviewed unfairly, in which case put it down to experience and scratch one interviewer off your party-invitation list. After "Yes", most interviewers will ease off a little.

Alternatively, the hostility may be unfounded. You've never laid anybody off, your investment product does deliver value for money, your cars aren't clunkers, et cetera.

If the hostile interviewer is just plain wrong, believe me, you're very lucky. You're being handed the chance really to assert your position, to defend it as strongly as you like, and bluntly, to win an argument in which you are absolutely in the right. Don't get angry, but don't back down either. Make your case forcefully. Make it well.

Put out of your mind the thought that the interviewer is probably only being hostile to get you to talk.

Here's an assertion that's been made already. You may not want to test it, but you can be sure that challenging interviews are often more successful than the all-friends-together variety.

Silence

You give your answer and the journalist appears to be waiting for something more. So, unless you've had a lot of experience at this, you say something else. Will this complete your answer? No. The journalist waits. You think: what have I missed? What else should I say?

By now you're way off your prepared line, and if you're not careful, you're going to start saying things you didn't intend to say.

That's the idea. In a conversation, people generally try to fill silence. But this isn't a conversation. It's an interview. Journalists have ways of making you talk and silence is one of them.

People who are good at being interviewed are also good at giving their answer and then stopping and waiting for the next question. When there's a silence, some of them even smile, as if to say, I know what you're doing.

Why?

Here's one of those questions that a journalist can throw into an interview just to shake things up a bit. Why? Is that really true? Are you sure? Really?

When you get one of these questions, answer briefly. What do you mean, why? Yes, it is really true. I am sure. Yes, really.

Don't go back over your previous answer and try to expand it, explain it or justify it. If you see an opportunity, say something new. But don't be knocked off balance by the unexpected question.

The totally idiotic follow-up question

This is sometimes a trick. Sometimes, it's what you get when the journalist has spent your previous answer not only nodding at you, not only saying "Uh huh" at intervals, but also thinking, "Is the tape recorder running? Should I have replaced the batteries? Am I going to run out of questions? Does he realise how little I know about all this?"

Either way, the totally idiotic follow-up question should be taken as an opportunity to say something that the questions so far haven't given you an opportunity to say. Ideally, your answer should connect, however tenuously, with the question. Ideally, you should conceal your view that the totally idiotic follow-up question is totally idiotic.

If you're on TV/radio, and it's live, the important thing is to keep talking. And not to let on that you think the journalist is an idiot. That will come across as arrogance. So just say something that you want to say. Confidently. With a straight face.

The stunningly ignorant question

Sometimes, a question will reveal to you that the journalist knows nothing whatsoever about the subject of the interview. If it's a live broadcast, keep talking and remember that you're talking to the audience as well as the journalist; they are the ones who matter, and they should understand what you're on about. Comments made in the section above also apply here.

The alternative approach, given that your aim is not to make the journalist feel like an idiot but to get written up as a generous, helpful, approachable kind of guy, is to say something like, "Let me put this in context …" or even, "Before I can answer that, I need to give you some background." Then you explain, as tactfully as possible, that two and two make four. You might want to drop in the occasional, "As you know…" and if possible, try to get through the whole explanation without it becoming too obvious that you've gone into teaching-the-basics mode.

Don't be caught out, either. Journalists aren't always as ignorant as they seem. Sometimes they're pretending ignorance just to get you to say something quotable.

Horizontal ignorance

On behalf of journalists everywhere, here's the big excuse. Journalists are rarely subject specialists. On a management magazine, for example, they might be writing about MBA programmes one month, customer-relationship management the next, and then perhaps cross-cultural marketing challenges the month after that. There isn't enough time and there aren't enough staff on any title for one person to dedicate a professional life exclusively to one subject.

You, however, are a subject specialist. You have been working in your subject area for long enough to be worth interviewing about it. You know the answers, and you even know the right questions to ask. If we had a flipchart to hand, we might draw a vertical line (perhaps more than one) to indicate, first, your area(s) of expertise and, secondly, the fact that you've got them covered top to bottom.

Now let's draw a line on the flip chart to indicate the journalist's areas of expertise. It's pretty much horizontal. It goes into a whole range of areas, but you couldn't really say that it's deep in any of them. It would look good if we extended it to cover research skills, interview skills, et cetera, but in terms of subject matter, the skill that counts for a journalist is knowing enough to know what he doesn't know.

The technology breaks down

Once upon a time, many years ago, people used slide projectors rather than PowerPoint and its successors for their presentations. In those days, slides would often be upside-down or backwards, or they'd get stuck in the projector and melt.

The rule always was: you could either be embarrassed about it, and lose the audience's sympathy, or you could get the audience on your side against the technology.

The same applies these days. If you're planning to use technology in a presentation to journalists, the rules are:

1   Don't.

2   If you do, have a back-up plan.

Once, a bank gave a PowerPoint presentation to a group of journalists. They started by lowering the shutters over the windows using a remote control. As the shutters came down, one journalist was heard muttering, "Please stop, please break!"

Because the bank was very pleased with its new remote-control shutters, and seeking to impress, we might state a principle thus:

> If you're trying to impress journalists, and being too obvious about it, they will try very hard not to be impressed.

If the journalist's own technology breaks down, take the opportunity to be generous and helpful. You're a nice person, after all.

That's it for tricks. Now we move on to discuss the various different interactions you might have with journalists.

Telephone calls

We'll start with the **unexpected telephone call**. This is the one where the journalist needs a quote now rather than to arrange an interview later. It's worth a mention because an unexpected journalist is often a journalist in search of a new contact, or a journalist who's realised at the last minute that she's short of a detail, or a quote, on a key point of her story. Either way, this is the opportunity to test your media-handling arrangements, and to demonstrate your accessibility. Either way, you're on trial: are you worth having as a contact at all; are you a contact who's willing to help out in a crunch? If you can't take the call, either return it as soon as you can, or make sure that the journalist understands that you really are unavailable. Ideally, there should be somebody else in the office briefed to take the call in your absence.

Where you've got a **prearranged telephone interview** coming up, get the team together in advance. If you want somebody else sitting in on the call, get them in before time. Don't have a journalist holding while somebody goes and finds So-and-so. As a general observation, conference calls are preferable to putting a journalist on speakerphone.

Minor point. Try to cut out background noise. When somebody else is speaking, don't hold the mouthpiece to your mouth. Listening to other people's breathing is bad for the concentration.

As a general rule, the technical terminology is always attractive to a journalist, as are the acronyms. But both can be surprisingly difficult to hear accurately on playback. Without being too obvious about it, take them slowly, and perhaps spell out the acronyms. If a journalist can throw in occasional casual references to the EBRD, the price-to-book ratio, the Fed rate, MRSA, the Doppler effect, Schlanger's paradigm and maybe even Schrodinger's cat, she'll be grateful to you for the opportunity to sound as though she knows more than she's putting into the story. But it's really annoying to interview people who use really interesting words and acronyms, but don't enunciate them clearly enough to transcribe accurately. You can't mention the MBNU if you're uneasy that it might be the MPNU.

Any good journalist will ask you for your name and your job title at the beginning or the end of a telephone interview. This is not necessarily because she doesn't know who you are. It is because recorded interviews can be put on one side and not used until a week later (it's unusual for a journalist to be working on one story at a time; probably she'll be finishing one while she does the interviews for the next). A voice on tape could be anybody. A voice saying your name, your title and your company, as you'd like to be quoted, is unmistakably you.

In a prearranged telephone interview, don't waste time. Offering to fill in the background, or put an answer in context, or whatever, can be an effective way of breaking the ice, and you can take the opportunity to slot in one or two hints as to angles the journalist might like to pursue. But even if you're asked to begin by saying a few words about your company, make it brief. This is just the warm-up. It's not the game.

 Last word on telephone calls. It's very easy for the journalist to put down the phone and ring somebody else. Given the point made earlier that no journalist researches a feature by interviewing just one person, she'll have a list of alternative contacts ready to hand. You're dealing with somebody whose tolerance for hold music is very low.

The role of PR in an interview

In an interview, the role of PR is to handle the nuisance stuff, fend off interruptions, follow through on promises (delivering the promised mugshot, for example), serve the coffee, order the wine, get the bill, deal with the coffee you've just knocked over, ask the occasional prompt question ("Wasn't there something you wanted to say about the new model's safety features, Bill?"), make the introductions, make sure the business card and the press pack get handed over, write up a short note (immediately) afterwards summarising the key points as you would like them to be remembered and dropping in all the useful acronyms.

PRs can ring five minutes before the due time for a conference call to check that the journalist hasn't forgotten about it, and they're quite useful if you want to know a bit more about a journalist in advance. Don't, however, judge them on their grasp of your industry. Their function is to provide you with uninterrupted access to the journalist so that you can do the talking. They're not there to do the talking for you.

Interviews in person

These can take any one of a number of forms, some of which we'll address in separate sections following this one. The principle common to all of them is that, as stated earlier, you're on show from the very first contact with the journalist. First and last impressions count. And because it's very much easier to be off your guard with somebody who's packing up to go, remember this:

Anything you say to a journalist might be quoted.

The unguarded remark in the lift going back down to reception; the answer to the question about what you're doing at the weekend; the casual exchange with a colleague in passing – it's all potentially part of the story.

This is because stories – particularly long magazine features – tend to read better if the people in them come across as human. Don't clam up completely once you've delivered your message, but keep your brain in gear. There's nothing wrong with talking about what you're going to do at the weekend, and it might deepen the relationship to do so, but if you're planning to spend the weekend robbing a bank, be circumspect.

One-to-one briefings over coffee and an agenda

If you're hosting a day-long series of briefings for individual journalists, one after another, don't have the agenda on the table in front of you. They can all read upside-down, and they'll all want to know most of all who gets the lunch and who just gets coffee.

If this is a briefing at your invitation, on your territory (whether this is your office or a neutral location such as a hotel), the onus is on you to keep talking. They're here because you invited them, not because they've been hoping for a chance to ask you a few questions. Also, to get them out of their offices your PR people have probably had to make one or two commitments about, let's say, the exciting announcement you're planning to make. Give your guests a good excuse for the time you've spent away from the office.

Minor housekeeping point: don't be clearing away the previous journalist's coffee cup when the next one arrives. Don't say, "I won't, I've just had one." You don't have to drink everything you accept.

One-to-one briefings will tend to be mediated by PR people, not least because the scope for losing journalists in the corridors is that little bit higher. Also, if possible, it is a good idea not to let incoming and outgoing journalists compare notes. The answer to, "What's this all about, then?" in reception might be more memorable than your version.

One-to-one briefings of this kind are a useful mechanism for simultaneously releasing news that different titles will treat in different ways. The technical magazine, for example, can be accommodated in the same morning as the Sunday business pages and the thirty-second radio slot. Good practice is to have an idea in advance of a different angle on the story for each journalist expected.

But above all, keep talking.

Lunch

There is never a time when it is a bad idea to spring an item of news on a journalist, and lunch is no exception. Always feel free to let slip a major exclusive.

That said, lunch with an individual journalist will tend to be more of a getting-to-know-you exercise than a formal interview; more of an overview than a trawl through the technical data. You can't expect your guest to scribble frantically as his Haddock Mornay goes cold on his plate, any more than you can serve three of the greatest wines made this century and then expect your explanation of the precise application of the Sharpe ratio to investment decision-making to be reproduced verbatim in tomorrow's paper.

> **By the way, about the only universally applicable rule about alcohol and the media is: don't get more drunk than the journalist(s).**

You can use lunch to demonstrate that you really do understand the major issues of the day, or you can spend it sidling round to such tricky questions as why they never mention your company. You can wax lyrical about why you really like this business you're in, or you can just take the opportunity to spend a few hours away from the office in congenial company. What you can't expect to do terribly successfully across the lunch table is, for example, launch a new product.

If you find yourself booked to eat lunch with an influential but complete stranger, do some research. This will entail more than just asking a few questions. You may not use your knowledge, but it's useful, for example, to have read a few pieces by the person facing you across the table. It's useful to hear more than just the fact that your PR person thinks the two of you will get on well together. Why? If the guy is going to spend lunch digging for diary items, that's worth knowing too.

Unless there is something delicate to discuss (you're thinking of reshuffling your cabinet and you want the press to know about it first), you may find it helpful to be accompanied to lunch by your PR person. This is partly because the PR person can be handed the wine list and told to get on with it, but also partly because the PR person will have a clear idea of what the lunch is supposed to achieve. You and your new friend might settle into a lengthy exchange of views on fly fishing, but your PR person will know very well that he earns his fee only if the journalist leaves the restaurant not only clutching the press pack but also remembering your name and what you do for a living.

It may be that you really do have to leave before the coffee is served, but if the lunch is going well and you feel you really have achieved an understanding, give at least a moment's thought to calling and cancelling your two o'clock. Small point, but, y'know, think about it.

Press conferences

You get several dozen people into a room who know each other professionally but don't often get the chance to exchange trade gossip. Then you try to interrupt their conversation with your announcement. That's how press conferences can sometimes feel to the attending journalists.

Press conferences are probably best used for big public announcements where there isn't much scope for in-depth questioning (or they may be used for group briefings where you're not planning to grant exclusives). They may be used in conjunction with scheduled one-to-ones after the main conference, but the general principle is: you won't get journalists asking their really perceptive questions in front of their colleagues, for fear of losing their exclusive angle. Sometimes, therefore, a journalist who is interested by your announcement may not take the opportunity to ask his big question, and may never get round to following it up later.

If you are planning to hold a press conference, there is one serious and one not-so-serious consideration to take into account:

- The journalists at your press conference may share their opinions over the coffee/lunch/drinks afterwards, and may reach a consensus view that is reflected in the ensuing coverage. It may be worth having members of staff circulating who can pick up on any misunderstandings, et cetera. Do remember, however, that journalists enjoy talking shop and may feel inhibited from doing so while your people are within hearing range.

- On a less serious note, journalists do tend to know who provides the best sandwiches, et cetera, at their press conferences. Not that this is an important point, but if you discover that your biggest rival served cardboard sandwiches to the same media audience last week, you might think it worth phoning the caterers to improve your own offering. Might give you an edge…

Press conferences are a very good way of getting straightforward information out quickly to a large media audience, and for this reason they are a useful tool in crisis management (Chapter 7). It is generally sensible for questions to be mediated from a central point, and for the chairperson to invite questions and distribute them.

However, and this is particularly true in a crisis, you should not fall into the trap of (possibly unintentionally) limiting questions to questions from the floor. It should be clear that those on the platform will be available for questions afterwards, and it should be possible for follow-up appointments to be made where there is a queue (scrum) of journalists around a single person.

Where a press conference is to be attended by senior staff who do not typically come into contact with the media, there may be a good case for providing them with at least some informal media training beforehand. The trappings of seniority in an organisation are not necessarily a good preparation for contact with today's media pack.

Round-table discussions, wine-tastings and other gimmickry

It is a good thing to entertain journalists. Nothing said in this section is intended to suggest otherwise. However, media entertaining is done badly at least as often as it is done well.

If you are going to invite, say, a dozen trade journalists to a round-table dinner and discussion on the future of your industry, here are some key points:

- They don't work in your industry. They work in the media.

- They stop thinking about your industry when they knock off work.

- Most of them probably want to talk to each other at least as much as they want to talk to you.

- Oh, and if you are going to start making speeches and presentations, you might want to make sure the wine is open and within reach.

If you are going to invite journalists to a wine tasting, casino evening, go-kart race, seasonal media party or other festivity, here are some more points:

- Some of them will enjoy the gimmick. Almost all of them will want to network with each other.

- Somebody else threw a party rather like this one just last week, except they also had clowns and a fire-eating juggler.

- They know you're delighted to see them. They know your company welcomes the opportunity to get to know its friends in the media in an informal setting. They know this is a chance to get to know the colleagues you've brought along with you. Siddown.

Take any advice you can get from your PR people on which journalist likes what kind of event. Vary the mix a little. And don't automatically assume that every journalist needs to take home a heavy desk diary, or another paperweight. Pens are useful, as are notebooks and gadgets, but if it's going to be expensive jewellery, could the logo be easy to peel off, please?

Dealing with members of the public

You may find yourself dealing directly with members of the public in a media context, for example in a radio phone-in such as *Moneybox Live*.

The rules here are very simple. Never, ever embarrass them. Never let them feel that they've asked a stupid question. Make them feel good about the conversation they're having with you. Don't overdo the flattery, but make it obvious that you take them seriously.

This is only partly because the audience will identify with the member of the public before they identify with you. More important is that in such a context, most of the audience won't be interested in any particular answer. Most of the time, therefore, your answers will hold only (say) ten per cent of the audience spellbound because that's exactly the answer they need. For the rest of the audience, who are listening because they like this programme and because you might say something interesting later, you will be conveying an impression of expertise rather than the expertise itself.

The ideal thought process in the audience's collective mind should be that you're kind, considerate, et cetera, and above all approachable with the questions they have to ask. They will take it for granted, because you're on the show, that you know what you're talking about.

And finally … all media contact ends when it ends

You've done the interview, held the press conference, fielded the Q&A, sat still while they unhooked the microphone. Now you're relaxing. This is your opportunity to blow the whole thing.

If you were an actor, the advice would be: stay in character. If there's any chance that there are still journalists anywhere near you, or that any of the recording equipment is still switched on, don't say, "Of course, it's not a new idea, really, but you've got to say something." Don't start poking fun at the silly questions asked at the press conference. Don't talk about how badly the company is doing, or how the board wants to get rid of the chairman, or whatever. Journalists don't go off duty just because you're off duty.

Once, a journalist interviewed a company director for a profile. The company's PR man sat in on the interview. Half-way through the interview, the journalist excused herself for a moment. Without thinking, she left her tape recorder running on the table. And the two men didn't notice it.

So when the journalist got back to her office, she was able to listen to what they'd said about her in her absence. In fact, back in the editorial office we all listened to it.

Stay alert. Don't make the stupid mistakes.

5

Television And Radio

Introduction

Everything said so far in this book applies equally to print and broadcast interviews. This is the chapter where we discuss the unique challenges of the broadcast interview.

The first thing to know about broadcasting is that the people doing it have a lot more to worry about than just interviewing you. A print journalist could get through an interview with the back of an envelope and a blunt pencil (although he might prefer a digital recorder and just possibly shorthand). The result can be typed in, laid to page and sent to the printers fairly quickly. But a broadcast journalist has to contend with all the technology, technicians and paraphernalia required to record your words and then mix them into a package and get them on air.

Broadcasting tends to make journalists obsessive about two things: the timing of everything; and the quality (as in technical quality) of their recordings. Remember, for them, the words you say in interview make up a recording that may have to be broadcast. They're more than just raw material. If you multiply the amount of broadcasting equipment that could go wrong, by the number of people who have to do their bit between now and going on air, and then divide the answer by the time left before broadcast, you come up with an answer that indicates why, for example, radio people tend to spend whole interviews checking their recorders, and TV people seem far more worried about sound and light levels and the proper positioning of microphones than in absorbing the wisdom of what you're saying.

Your interview will also be timed to the second. If it's live, you won't have, let's say, a couple of minutes and then maybe ten seconds to wrap up if you're finishing an answer. If you're over-running, you will be interrupted. If you're being recorded, the sound bites used might not be more than a few seconds long. For broadcast, get into the habit of making your best points first and short.

It is possible that you will encounter broadcast journalists who are businesslike and well-informed and obviously understand what you're talking about. It is also possible that the programme is being put together by somebody else, in a hurry, and that the person sent to interview you is inadequately briefed, borrowed from a wildlife programme, and in a hurry to complete six interviews in two hours.

It is possible that you will encounter broadcast journalists who are humble, modest, respectful, grateful for your time. It is also possible that you won't. You may also come to understand, as your side-career in broadcasting continues, that some presenters are hired for their looks, or their voices, and not for their in-depth understanding of the minutiae of business. Don't get irritated with this. They don't mean anything. They're in a hurry, and anyway, your concern is to look/sound good in the final result.

First rule of broadcasting: remain calm. Second rule: you're in charge of your own contribution even if you can't control anything else. They may not know exactly what they want, and they may even make it difficult for you to deliver, asking ill-informed questions, changing the running order of a live broadcast at the last second, thrusting a powder-puff into your face just as you're focusing on your breathing and trying to meditate to reduce the stress of it all.

But as long as you've got your sound bites ready, as long as you understand that looking good and sounding good matter more than feeling obligated to answer a stupid question, you should find broadcasting a lot easier than you might expect.

Covered in this chapter:

- Preparing for a broadcast interview

- Nerves

- Staying in position

- Live, as-live and recorded interviews

- Hostility

- Simplicity

- Your objectives in a broadcast interview

- Television comes to the office

- You go to the TV studio

- You're invited to a remote studio

- Radio comes to the office

- You go to the radio studio

- Phone-ins and being interviewed over the phone

- Drying

- And finally … post-microphone depression

Preparing for a broadcast interview

One big difference between print and broadcast journalists is that while the print people will tend to resist being tied down to a fixed list of questions, broadcast people will want to tie you down to a narrow focus on a specific angle in advance. The print people can tie it all into an angle later; with a broadcast, it's the words you actually say that are going out on air. So they've got to be the right words.

What this means is that you can expect a lengthier process of pre-interview negotiations, possibly running across more than one phone call, in advance of your encounter with the interviewer. This may not happen (sometimes, it might not happen simply because time is short), and when it does happen, you may be talking to a researcher rather than the person who will be interviewing you. (In any pre-interview conversation, if you're going to a studio check the details of when, where, and crucially, who to ask for at the door – more on this below.)

With a recorded interview, some of the getting-the-words-right discussion can happen during the interview itself ("Could you say that again, but leave out the joke about the elephant in the room"), but with a live interview, you might find yourself talking to a researcher, then the programme's forward-planners, then the people actually making the programme, then somebody who shows you the way to the waiting room, then the person doing the interview … and then you'll do the interview. Which might last a minute.

There are three things to know about pre-interview negotiations.

1   **What you say, and what they say, will be the basis for the interview.** Listen. If the researcher says, "So you could talk about the oil-refinery fire in the Ukraine?" You can be sure you'll get a question about it. These are people who, when they're not in a hurry, act as though they're in a hurry, so although it may sound as though you're having a quick preliminary chat, you're actually agreeing the detailed interview plan.

2   **It is always a bad idea to rehearse your answers in advance.** Don't "perform" in the pre-interview negotiations, and never fall into the trap of trying to repeat what you said then in the actual interview. Spontaneous is good.

3   **Actual interviews follow their own logic.** The interviewer might depart from the list of questions, or not have paid attention to the brief, or be so struck by something you say that he goes off at a tangent to follow it up. Don't be surprised if you're taken by surprise.

If you want to be asked back, don't ask for a list of questions to be sent over in advance, and if you do ask, don't be surprised if the questions you're asked in the interview don't match the questions on the sheet. Broadcasters have a high tolerance for behind-the-scenes chaos and a very low tolerance for memos, paperwork and bureaucracy.

For radio, wear what you like but don't bring your preparatory notes to the studio. For television, ideally don't wear light-to-mid blue shirts, blouses, et cetera, because that's the colour of the screen behind you, onto which they project the background graphics (the risk is that the blue part of you merges with the background) and avoid complex patterns, stripes and checks that might "run" on camera (the newer their technology, the less likely this is to be a problem, but it's still worth bearing in mind). A grey suit is preferable to a black suit (which will be a flat expanse of non-colour). And don't bring your preparatory notes. You won't come across well if you're struggling to read something from the notes in front of you, rather than talking directly to the interviewer.

If you're going to a studio, turn up early. There will be a lot of security, and in a large broadcasting organisation, it is conceivable that the person at reception will not be able to find you on the day's list of guests. It is possible that this is because the very busy person who booked you overlooked one detail – telling the desk you were coming. It is prudent to have the name and extension number (perhaps also mobile number) of the person who is expecting you.

> Note: There may be senior people working on the programme who won't recognise your name – bring the right contact name and extension number.

You can ask for a taxi to be arranged to bring you to the studio, but don't rely on it turning up or the driver recognising the address or knowing the way. Do remember either to ask for a taxi to take you back to the office, or to ask the taxi to wait.

In the immediate run-up to a broadcast interview that is happening at a studio rather than on your own territory, you may be on the receiving end of a lot of TLC (tender loving care) and attention. This is a good moment to clear any minor worries you might have (it's a tense time: questions asked at such moments include, do I address the interviewer by his first name, and, how will he know my name?) and of course it is designed to relax you as well as to get an impression of you. So try to relax. But don't talk about the interview, and especially not about what you're going to say. It's possible that your interviewer will have a moment to slip out of the studio and say hello, but again, don't say anything you're going to want to repeat on air.

Oh, and turn off your mobile and anything else that might bleep at the wrong moment.

Nerves

Not much to say about this. Nerves are good, to the extent that they charge you up and get your adrenalin running. If you weren't nervous, you wouldn't be primed to give an exciting, lively interview.

Getting too nervous is often something you do to yourself. If that's happening, the thing you're probably doing wrong is thinking too much about the interview. So be ready to distract yourself. You probably won't be in the mood to read a novel, but you could probably teach yourself origami, or sew on a button, or carve a balsa wood hippopotamus in a dressing room.

Alcohol? No. Unless you find that it works to prime yourself for board meetings with a swift half, don't do it for TV and radio.

Staying in position

You've got your head straight and you're ready to go. Somebody leans over your shoulder and tells you to keep your mouth … this close … to the microphone. So you spend the interview fixed in position, worrying about the microphone.

Be ready for that one. On radio, it's not your job to worry about the microphone, although it is a good idea not to move around too much. They'll position the microphone on the basis of where you're sitting, and after that, you can forget about the microphone and get on with the interview. If you do forget that you're not supposed to change your position by more than a few inches, let them sort it out.

On television, you'll be placed within shot of one or more cameras. As long as you don't stand up and walk off somewhere else, you will have freedom of movement. Don't wave your arms too much, or remain totally still. Don't put your hands in front of your face. Ideally, don't lean right back one moment and then sit far forward the next. The conventional advice for this situation is: be natural.

If you're wearing one of those little clip-on microphones, try not to move in such a way that, for example, it slips in behind the lapel of your jacket. At the end of the interview, expect everybody to say simultaneously, "Mind the microphone!" rather than, "Thank you very much".

Live, as-live and recorded interviews

In a live broadcast, talk. Remember that the audience will get (almost) as much from your tone of voice and your appearance, as from what you actually say. From looking at you and/or hearing you, they will gather enough information to be able to conclude: the subject of this interview is – whatever – and this person knows all there is to know about it. That's enough, frankly.

In a live broadcast, be in control. If they get your name wrong, correct it. If you start a sentence badly, say something like, "Let me say that again," and say it again. The audience will be on your side throughout, on the single condition that they don't catch you in an attempt to conceal anything, including nerves.

If the interview is recorded, you can afford to relax a bit more, although bear in mind that an interviewee who doesn't need editing will be more popular than an interviewee who does. Sometimes, you might be told that an interview is being recorded "as live", which might mean that they want to record as much of a programme as possible in one take. Treat such an interview as live.

Hostility

Towards the beginning of this book, in Chapter 1, you are advised to read, watch or listen to the journalists who might one day be interviewing you. Once you have done this, you will be in a position to put together a list of interviewers, and indeed programmes, whose invitations you would be prudent not to accept. There are radio and television programmes that specialise in disapproval, to put it mildly, just as there are interviewers whose style amounts to portraying featured individuals in a bad light.

There are also some consumer-affairs programmes that like to challenge companies on behalf of one or more aggrieved consumers. Ask a lot of questions and do a lot of homework before going on such a programme (and if you do, never be hostile to a member of the public; see Chapter 4).

This book is not going to suggest that you accept every invitation. Turn some of them down. But there's something more important to say about hostility: you will almost certainly not encounter any. Unless hostility is part of the brief, as it would be for programmes such as those just described, broadcast journalists typically embark on research open-minded. They're looking for an angle on their subject, and if they find one, they will run with it. There isn't time to do otherwise.

So don't go into an interview expecting hostility. But if you do find yourself in a studio facing somebody who is clearly not on your side, fight back. If you're in the right, say so. A tough interview can come out better than an easy ride, not least because you'll be fired up. Don't lose your temper, never lose your self-control, but don't back down.

If you are in the wrong, you might have to express regret. Or answer a different question from the one asked ("Good question, but the real issue here is …"). Or, if you can reach and won't be spotted, pull the microphone cable out of the wall. The worst move, always, is to be evasive. Never, ever, avoid a question or deny the obvious. If you're evasive, you're trying to deceive the audience, and that always goes down very badly indeed.

Simplicity

In a broadcast interview, radio or television, the audience does not have time to think. They can't read a paragraph again, for example, or sit back and consider what they've just read before reading on to the end (they might be able to download a programme, but plan for the majority who won't).

The audience is also much less targeted. It may be larger, and it may contain many more of your potential customers than you could reach through, say, a trade magazine, but it is safe to assume that they aren't listening and/or watching with the same attention as they might bring to a specialist print publication such as a trade magazine.

On television and radio, keep it simple. There just won't be time, and the audience isn't paying enough attention, to get into the complexities of anything. To use a print analogy, speak in headlines and introductory paragraphs. Reflect also on what a casual listener or viewer will remember of your contribution. Some of it will be what you say. But a lot of it will have to do with the sound of your voice and your appearance. Be confident, interested and enthusiastic.

Your objectives in a broadcast interview

Next, we will look in detail at some of the broadcast experiences you might face. But first, let's set you up with some objectives. (This section groups together key points made briefly in passing elsewhere in this chapter.)

What do you want to get from a broadcast interview? The answer might be easy. Let's see … name recognition, a higher profile, consumer awareness, experience, a new heading for the CV, perhaps even practice for the day on which you can't avoid a broadcast interview that really is make or break? Perhaps all of the above; perhaps you have other objectives; perhaps the broadcast interview is a by-product of, say, a results announcement or a new launch.

No. Whatever you're doing in front of the microphone, your first and most immediate objective should be very narrow and very simple: to come across well.

Of course, you need to get your message across. There are numbers that need to be disclosed, say, and perhaps the name of the new product needs to be repeated as frequently as possible. But whatever you're doing, consider three things:

1   On **radio**, listeners will judge you at least as much (and almost certainly more) by your tone of voice as by what you say. Some listeners will listen to you; all of them, listening or not, will be likely to think something along the lines of, "He sounds friendly," or indeed, "He sounds nervous."

2   On **television**, viewers will form an impression based on your appearance and tone of voice. It's no good having a perfect interview in your notes, if you deliver your sound bites as though you're guilty and expecting to be unmasked at any moment.

3   On both **radio and television**, the impression you give, your attitude, enthusiasm, tone of voice, etc., will be what is memorable. Even those who pay close attention to your words, who are your target audience for the interview, will remember what you said in the light of how you said it.

This is intended to be reassuring. You do not have to go into the studio worrying that you are going to be asked a question that you can't answer. You don't have to worry about not having time to get across every last technicality. This isn't the interviewer's interview. This is your interview. You are going to be expressing yourself directly through the screen/loudspeaker to the proverbial audience at home. What matters, because that audience will first and foremost be responding to your appearance/tone of voice, is that you relax and do this your way. Be yourself. Or failing that, be the person you want them to think you are.

Here is a reaction that the audience will not have:

"Hang on. He was asked about the weather in general and he started talking about rainfall patterns. That's outrageous!"

Here is a reaction that the audience might have:

"I like the sound of this person. Certainly knows everything about not getting soaked in a shower. Come to think of it, maybe I need a new umbrella."

And so on through whatever imaginary conversations you care to invent. But while we're on the subject of weather, how often do you listen to a weather forecast, even if you've tuned in to hear it, and come away with a clear understanding of where the isobars are all going? My guess? Not as often as you come away thinking that you like, dislike, or want to argue with the forecaster.

It would be nice if your answers bore some relevance to the subject under discussion. It would be polite if you were to answer the interviewer's questions. But the impression that the audience will take away is what really matters. Your objective, therefore, is to sound, and look, both convincing and approachable.

Now let's put you through some interviews.

Television comes to the office

If a camera crew is expected at your office, spend some time thinking about background. You might want to be filmed sitting in front of a plant (don't have it behind you and looking as though it's growing out of your head), or perhaps standing in front of a busy dealing room, or perhaps just sitting at your desk. You might judge it appropriate to stand in front of a wall on which your company logo can be seen (don't overdo this, and if that means standing in reception, judge how irritated the camera crew is going to get with constant interruptions from visitors). If your choice of background includes people sitting at their desks, you might want to clear this with them in advance; they might, for example, want to check that they're looking their best before appearing on television.

Your interviewer will want to make her own mind up about where to put you, and it is generally prudent to reach a friendly agreement on this point. If the company logo is bigger than you are, and you insist on standing in front of it, you might not be shown on screen, for example. Also, the camera man might have a view on lighting; there's also background noise to consider, et cetera.

Let them get on with this. You're the target of the exercise rather than a member of the team. At some point, they will start moving the furniture. They will probably want to be shown where the plug sockets are, and if you can lay on coffee and biscuits, great. They will always need more space.

> **As a general rule, and unless there's an obvious producer, the interviewer is your first point of contact in a camera crew.**

As to business cards, the interviewer will need one, and if the opportunity arises, try to get one across to the camera man. He's the one responsible for the film clips of you talking, and if they get edited and delivered with your name attached, correctly spelled, so much the better.

Don't expect anybody in the crew, except the interviewer, to know who you are or why they're there.

A camera crew might consist of an interviewer and somebody to hold the camera. Or you might find yourself facing an interviewer, cameraman, sound recordist, person with clipboard, younger person without clipboard, person in combat gear plugging things into each other and a work-experience person. Camera crews are often freelance outfits with friends who come along to help carry the bags.

The crew's equipment might consist of a small digital camera and a clip-on microphone. Or there might be a big camera, lights, TV monitor, boom microphone, clip-on for back-up, boxes with cables coming out of them and various shoulder-bags with more cables rolled up inside them. Some of it might belong to the TV station, or it might be hired. There's always a budget for equipment hire, and sometimes, the freelances can spend less by hiring older, bigger equipment.

There is usually a faint atmosphere of disciplined, efficient chaos about a camera crew. They know what they're doing, but the equipment has been used a hundred times before and can break down. The camera's batteries haven't been charged. There's a crucial cable missing from the box. Problems tend to be solved by a combination of mobile phones, taxis, cash and sending the person in combat gear to find the nearest tech store.

Before the interview, they will want you in place talking about nothing. Tell them what you had for breakfast. Don't say anything you wouldn't want quoted. They're checking that the camera is working and the sound is recording, but they'll see this again when they edit. The US president who sound-checked with the words, "The missiles are flying," came to regret it.

How do you handle the interview? First, establish whether you should look at the camera or at the interviewer (probably the latter). Then relax. They've spent budget on sending these people and this equipment to your office. They want you to succeed. This is a recorded interview, so they can edit out your mistakes (if there's time). With an experienced interviewer, who is also producing the package, you might even be coaxed through your answers ("Could you say that again, but this time, lean slightly forward?").

You might want to discuss questions, even suggest questions, although don't fall into the trap of giving your answers before you actually give them. ("Would you like me to say … ?")

As usual, the rule is:

the more you talk, the better you're doing.

Remember that in the finished broadcast, they probably won't use more than a few sentences of your interview at a time. You might appear more than once, but each time, you'll just be delivering a single sound bite.

So speak accordingly. In sentences. And if you fluff a line, start again at the beginning. If you realise that a sentence has too many ums and ahs in it, start again. Leave a short pause before a restarted sentence. The sound editor has a little squiggly line going across the computer screen in front of him. Where the line goes flat, that's a pause. Easy to spot a pause and cut it. Spotting an "um" in mid-sentence is more difficult.

At the end of the interview, they might want to film "cutaways". These might include shots of your hands, shots of the interviewer nodding at your answers, shots of the interviewer asking all the questions over again, shots of you listening to the questions (just pretend) and general shots of the office. They might want to record some of the ambient silence of the office, because your silence will be different from silence anywhere else and they might need to splice in the occasional brief interval. They might want to do a stand-up intro with the presenter inside or outside the office.

And that's it. Say goodbye, put the office back to normal, and get back to work.

You go to the TV studio

It's all arranged. You're going on the breakfast show to review the business pages. Or you're going in to be interviewed for a slot on your subject. Or you're going to be a talking head on a regular business programme (it's good experience and probably good for business, but think about the regular commitment).

Be prepared for any or all of the following:

- You turn up at reception. **The person behind the desk has never heard of you** and doubts that you really are expected. BUT you have brought the name of the person who booked you in, and her phone number. So that's okay.

  You turned up early, because you know this kind of thing happens.

- You're taken into **make-up**, where a young person powders your face so that it won't shine under the lights. Unless you have a particular aversion to make-up, you should submit to this (it washes off). If you're already wearing make-up, negotiate. The idea is to leave you with a matte finish.

You brought along a little mirror, so that you can check, at the last minute, that you haven't got powder on your suit. You also brought a comb.

- You're taken to a **dressing room** by a person who might be carrying a clip-board with the show's running order and might be wearing a headset. That person will need to know your name and your title and your company name. Give the whole lot in the form that you'd like it to appear on screen, under your face. If your name is difficult, spell it. If your title is long, abbreviate it or leave it out altogether. If you don't, they'll do it for you. There's only so much space for a caption.

- This person can also tell you where to go to wash your hands. Worth knowing that.

- **You'll be told when they'll be coming for you** and left in a dressing room. There might be other people in the room who are also going on the show. They might be people worth knowing. "We met in a TV studio" is a good start to a business relationship.

  Don't talk about what you're going to say. Talk about anything else.

- People are taken away at intervals. Then, suddenly, **it's your turn**. You're led down the corridor, through a door, and into a large, dark space. You're told not to trip over any of the cables. The person with the clipboard is waiting for an opportunity to take you onto the set. You feel very close to the person with the clipboard at this point.

- Then it's the ads, or they've switched to the local news, or they're playing a pre-recorded package. Whatever it is, it's the short break in transmission that gives the studio people time to play musical chairs. **You're led onto the set**. Somebody is led off. You might sit on a hard sofa. You might sit behind a plywood painted desk with the rest of the panel. There might be a mark on the desk to show you exactly where to sit to be in line with the camera. You might greet some of the people you met in the dressing room. The presenter introduces himself. You're shown your caption and somebody points to a camera, saying something about a red light that will come on when it's live. You see yourself in a monitor.

- This is when you take a deep breath, relax, and think about the last time you went snorkelling in the Caribbean. It is a very bad thing to think about what you're going to say. Don't rehearse any answers. If you've never been snorkelling in the Caribbean, make yourself a promise that on the way back to the office, you will stop at a travel agent.

The point about a TV studio is that everybody in it is very busy. The other point is that this close to transmission, they're working in seconds rather than minutes. By now, there's no time for anything except getting you on, interviewing you, and getting you off again. If it's any comfort, nobody in the studio will be paying attention to what you say. They'll be worrying about light, sound, timing, whatever is their specialist subject.

The presenter is talking out loud to somebody invisible (you realise, of course, that he's replying to the producer's voice in his earpiece). A disembodied voice says something about ten seconds. And then the presenter suddenly goes all avuncular and says, "Welcome back," to a point in the middle distance where there's a camera. Then he says, "we're joined by …" and in your peripheral vision, you see your face on a monitor.

Your eyes meet the presenter's eyes. He asks you a question.

And here's what you do:

- You keep a straight face. Look serious, interested, sincere.

- You look at the presenter.

- And you talk.

If you're lucky, the noises coming out of your mouth will resemble an answer to the question you've just been asked. But that's advanced stuff. What matters, in your first TV-studio interview, is that you produce coherent sentences in a tone of voice that conveys sincerity, et cetera.

In TV, the safety factor is that people are looking at you as well as listening to you. They're reacting to your appearance and the sound of your voice as well as to what you're saying. So you just have to say something.

And generally, the presenter is a professional presenter. He hasn't a clue what you're talking about, and because he read the question off a script, he probably wasn't even listening to the question while he was asking it. While he's nodding and looking interested in your answer, he's actually listening to a voice in his earpiece that might be saying, for example, "We've lost the live link to Brian in Washington, so we're going straight from this guy to the performing dog, then the panel discussion on closets and spin that out until the weather if we still can't get Brian. Okay, ask this guy the next question."

There will be somebody focussed on you, but what they'll be worrying about is whether or not you dry up completely. This is rare. It's rare because you're not tied to answering the question. That would be nice, but you're not obligated; this isn't an interrogation. If it happens, they might bring in somebody else on the sofa to express an opinion, or the presenter might say something (possibly dictated by the voice in his ear) or they might cut straight to the performing dog. If you dry up, get back into speaking mode as soon as you can. And afterwards, talk to your PR people about getting some media training sorted out.

You do your interview, and then you sit there until there's a break and somebody comes to take you away. You're led out of the studio. If you left anything in the changing room, you collect it. Then you leave.

Next stop, the travel agent.

You're invited to a remote studio

This might happen if your office is hundreds of miles from the studio where the programme is being made. There's no budget, nor is there time, to fly you to London, say, so you're directed to a remote studio nearer the office. If you ask, they'll provide a taxi, but – hint – they won't know your local taxi firms as well as you do.

A remote studio is a small, sound-proofed box containing a television camera, a monitor and a chair. It's like a sauna with technology instead of coals to provide the heat. There should also be a telephone. There may be a button to press (a power switch, as you come into the room) and a sheet of instructions. If you're lucky, there will be somebody nearby who has been commandeered to show you what to do.

The thing to remember about a remote studio is that it wasn't set up yesterday, especially for your interview. It was set up years ago, by TV people who hadn't really thought through the fact that it was going to be used by amateurs. Get there in good time, and don't expect anybody to be expecting you. Remote studios exist because TV companies can't afford full-scale studios everywhere; logically, therefore, they exist because TV companies can't afford to hire staff to sit around waiting for interviewees to turn up. It might be you and the work-experience person doing this together.

So you come in, you press the button, you read the instructions and you sit down. There may be an earpiece (and it may work). There may be a disembodied voice. On the monitor, you see the broadcast on which you're about to appear. The disembodied voice says, "Coming to you in ten," and you realise, by "you" they mean you.

By now, unless you've prepared yourself for this experience, you're a nervous wreck.

On the monitor, you can see the presenter introducing you. Suddenly, you see yourself gazing out of the screen. You hear a question.

Look at the camera.

Answer the question. At least, say something.

And then there's the next question, and the next. Then it's over.

Well done. And don't forget: turn off the power switch as you leave.

Radio comes to the office

Radio is less disruptive than television. If you're interviewed for radio at your office, the chances are you'll find yourself facing one person with a large microphone plugged into a small recording device. It may be that this person wears headphones for the interview; it may be that a second person also turns up.

Instead of thinking about background, as above, think about ambient noise. To state the obvious, radio people are primarily concerned with sound. If your office overlooks the M6, you might find yourself doing the interview in the broom cupboard on the other side of the building.

> **Alternatively, you might find yourself invited down to do the interview in the back of their van round the back of the building; this is unlikely unless we're talking about a live interview and you're so important that (a) the interview has to be done live now, and (b) you're too busy to travel to a studio.**

If you work in an environment where there are potentially interesting and/or relevant background noises, say so. The interviewer might welcome the opportunity to record, for example, the hum of the machinery or the rhythmic clicking of the, er, widgets. Such noises can provide, for example, an introduction to the package or a sound to be faded out at the end.

Radio people travelling with portable recording equipment tend to spend whole interviews adjusting dials and watching digital read-outs. They will be happy, if not actually eager, to allow you to repeat answers (unless it's already 12.30 and the programme goes out at 13.00) and they will want to play things back. They probably checked the equipment out that morning, and equally probably, the last person to use it didn't think to recharge the battery or report one or more faults.

Ums, ahs and re-started answers are okay (up to a point), but don't forget that a small pause between first and second attempts at an answer might be appreciated. Also don't forget that although your contribution might be edited, it might not be edited very well. Cutting out a large chunk that ends with the words, "Can I start that again?" will be easier than making sense of, "The, er, fact is, um, that, er, your question, well, your question, I mean, what it really, sort of, deserves, I think, in fact, what it needs is, um, a straight, sort of, really, a straight answer. Actually."

In any radio interview, your job is to talk. Be relevant if possible, but talk. Keep it simple, be enthusiastic, interested, whatever, but talk. In sentences. One point per answer. Talk, talk, talk.

You go to the radio studio

Radio studios tend to be functional, intimate spaces containing interviewers wearing headphones. They resemble TV studios in that you should turn up early and bring the name of the person who is expecting you. And the extension number. And the mobile number.

The pre-interview experience will tend to be similar to that described above in the section on going to a TV studio, except of course that you won't get the make-up. If you meet the interviewer/presenter in advance, or the producer, or just about anybody else, relax and chat but don't under any circumstances rehearse your answers in advance. You may hear the programme playing in the corridors.

Turn off your mobile phone and put your interview notes back in your briefcase. They'll rustle. If you try to read from notes in the interview, you'll sound like somebody trying to read from notes. Not being able to find the paragraph you want will add to your audible stress level.

You're taken into the studio at a convenient break. You're told where to sit and shown the microphone. You take a deep breath and the presenter completely ignores you. He's reading the running order to find out who you are. He might be having a conversation with somebody in the control room, which is behind glass.

And be prepared for this. If you've heard this presenter's voice on the radio before, especially if you're a regular listener, you will probably have formed some kind of a subliminal impression of his appearance. If you've never seen a photograph of the presenter, be prepared for the shock when you discover that the kindly, familiar, friendly voice you know so well actually comes out of somebody who has a physical appearance that you associate with something negative. We all make associations.

Radio presenters are hired because of what their voices "look like", not what they look like themselves. It's a detail, but you don't want surprises right now.

There may be time for a brief exchange with the presenter before your slot. There may be a chance to confirm your name and company name and what you're doing there.

Then it's your turn. This is what you do:

- You talk.

- You're concise.

- Short sentences.

- One sound bite per answer.

- You stop for the next question.

Unless and until you're experienced at this, there isn't time for much more than that. You might want to bring in an anecdote to support your answer, but make it brief. You might want to cite a statistic, but just one at a time, thank you.

There are programmes where there's scope for you to go on for quite a while, and there are interviews where you're in and out in less than a minute. Either way, the thing to avoid throughout is silence. You might want to pause for a split second to get yourself under control before you answer a question (indeed, this is suggested as a good idea elsewhere in this book), but what everybody wants you to do is talk.

Say what you like, as long as you talk.

Phone-ins and being interviewed over the phone

Telephones are bad news for broadcasters. The sound quality you get out of a telephone, land line or mobile, is not really good enough for broadcast, except where the person on the other end is a foreign correspondent speaking from a remote location or a member of the public.

It may happen one day that you are invited to join a panel of experts answering questions phoned in by members of the public. It may also happen one day that for whatever logistical reasons, you have to be interviewed over the phone from your office or your home. Occasionally, you may be on the phone answering phoned-in questions.

If you're the one on the phone, here's how to do it:

- Make absolutely sure you're not going to be interrupted.

- Hold the receiver at roughly 45 degrees to your mouth and talk across it.

- If you're listening rather than talking, don't breathe into the receiver.

- Remember that background noises can be heard.

If you are on that panel of experts answering questions, remember these points:

- Members of the public always ask good questions, even if they're so muddled and stupid that they're not directly answerable.

- The audience will (almost) always side with the member of the public.

- It's the presenter's job, not yours, to deal with any really impossible members of the public who get put through.

- It is a mistake to compete with other members of the panel, or to disagree except politely and in a spirit of friendly debate. If you can say, at least once but not too often, "I think that was a very good answer and may I add …" the audience will think you generous and you'll have a friend for life.

If you have a choice between going in to a studio and doing an interview over the phone, it is almost always better to go in to the studio.

Drying

This happens to very few people although a lot of people worry about it. If you have prepared yourself in advance, and then managed to put the whole thing out of your head in the minutes immediately before the interview, you should have kept your mind reasonably free of what-if-it-all-goes-horribly-wrong scenarios. Finding yourself unable to remember anything at all at precisely the moment you're asked a question live on national television – well, it's an experience not to repeat.

So don't over-think beforehand. If it does happen, be aware that the presenter will be working hard to help you out of it, or perhaps to shift attention away from you. Take a deep breath to reduce your heart rate. Keep doing this. When the opportunity arises, say something, even if it's only agreeing with something somebody else has said, just to break the ice.

If nothing works, put it down to experience. When the next opportunity arises, take it. Just because you dry once, doesn't mean you'll do it every time.

And finally ... post-microphone depression

Once you've been interviewed, everybody loses interest in you. On radio, you're led out of the studio and forgotten. If it was a telephone interview, the voice says thank you, and then you're listening to silence. Very rarely, the researcher might come on and thank you. But only very rarely. On television, they move on to the next interviewee and you're left hanging around the dressing room.

After the stress of being interviewed, this is a let-down. Be prepared for it. In particular, be prepared for finding yourself in an unfamiliar part of town. The best way to prepare for post-microphone depression is this: if they offer to send a car to collect you and bring you to the studio for the interview, insist that they provide a car to take you back to the office afterwards.

6

What Happens Next
And What More Can You Do?

Introduction

So you give your interview and say goodbye to the journalist. In this short chapter we take a look at what happens next. While you're getting back to the day job, what is the journalist doing and is there any way you could usefully nudge the process forward? Is there anything you really should do, or certainly shouldn't do, to increase your chances of favourable coverage?

Nine times out of ten, best advice on post-interview follow-up is: don't do it. Just sit by the phone (or at least, be contactable) in case the journalist needs anything else at the last minute. However, there can be occasions on which a carefully judged post-interview intervention can move your contribution from, let's say, low down on the second page to the opening paragraph of the feature.

There's also the question of when you might usefully get in touch to suggest a follow-up story and thus a further interview. We'll address that later in this chapter, although the immediate point to make is that if a journalist has just interviewed you about your subject, they're not going to be wanting another interview on the same subject immediately afterwards.

But first, how do you judge whether any given post-interview follow-up would have a positive outcome? To answer that question, let's start by looking at the end product. Take for example a daily newspaper. By the standards of most businesses, a daily newspaper is the product of a very rushed production process. First thing yesterday, today's paper didn't exist. Nor had it been planned in detail. Some of the features and some of the regulars were set up in advance, of course, but all of the news pages were empty. Any news they already had available was put into yesterday's paper. First thing yesterday, today's news pages were blank; there were no titles, no captions, no pictures, no market statistics. Just big rolls of blank paper.

And that's how they do it every day. A daily newspaper is a labour-intensive, capital-intensive, technology-dependent operation that starts out every day with twenty-four hours to design, build and distribute a new product. The journalists, along with the designers, editors, producers, researchers and presenters, are on the production line. Among the challenges they face are the unpredictability and (usually) inconvenient timing of major news events, and, for print titles, a fluctuating number of pages to fill (the availability of advertising being the significant determinant).

You can make the same point about radio and television: any edition of a daily news-based programme won't even have begun to take shape until after yesterday's edition was broadcast. Similarly, weekly and monthly publications don't get taken off the back burner until the previous issue is out of the way (although the less news-sensitive a title is, the more can be set up in advance – but come to think of it, it never seems to work out that way).

What does this mean to you?

The practical consideration is not only that journalists are very busy people (aren't we all?), but also that with non-negotiable deadlines to meet, when they are busy they have very little time indeed for distraction. They don't start work until the last minute – if you want to be sure you're covering the "latest" news, you can hardly start early – and once they do start working they do so as members of a team that is engaged in a highly pressurised, highly complex and significantly unpredictable process. They have to do their bit effectively and on time. Failure, as the saying goes, is not an option.

From this, we may draw a simple conclusion:

Journalists are only ever likely to be interested in inputs that carry their story forward.

If you can offer pictures, charts, case studies, exclusive interviews with key players who are available immediately: yes.

But if you want to get involved (or you want your PR person to get involved) in any follow-up relationship-management stuff about how was it for them, did they get everything they wanted, are there any further points, would they be interested in a guided tour of the factory, let's have lunch sometime, yada, yada, yada – kindly get off the phone.

As should be obvious, this is very important. Journalists are not always busy – sometimes they finish stories and relax – but they go to extremes: typically, they're either working at panic speed or chatting by the drinks machine.

Here's something else that's both obvious and important:

With any post-interview follow-up, you've got to get your timing right.

Later in this chapter, we'll discuss good times and bad times to call journalists, either for follow-up purposes or to suggest future stories. We'll also consider the typical journalist's capacity to retain the information you provide, and his likely attention span. But before we get to that, we need to talk a bit more about what will happen now to the interview you've just provided. What does the journalist do next?

Covered in this chapter:

- What happens to your interview?

- How does a journalist's memory work?

- How to deliver the follow-up

- So what about pictures?

- From one interview to the next

- When is a good time to call a journalist?

- And finally … when is a good time to be sitting by the phone?

What happens to your interview?

For practical purposes, although the technicalities will be different, the treatment of your interview will be the same whether you gave it to a print title or to a radio/TV programme. This is not a chapter about how to use page-layout software to bring together text, pictures, captions, charts, other stories, advertisements, et cetera into a readable-looking page, any more than we need to get into the complexities of combining sound bites, linking voice-overs, background music, ambient sound, pictures, talking heads holding microphones, passing members of the public waving to mum, into a convincing package. But listing the components of the product conveys something of the complexity of the process.

This is how it's done. Your words will be transcribed or edited so that instead of a tape recording and some scribbled notes, the end product of the interview becomes a set of coherent, grammatical quotes (print) or of hesitation-free, succinct, subject-verb-object sound bites (broadcast). The journalist will almost certainly want to collect quotes/sound bites from at least one other person, and it is likely that the angle of the story, and the questions asked in subsequent interviews, will be influenced by what you said in your interview.

Each interview will influence each subsequent interview. You got the point made earlier in the book, didn't you, about making your quotes punchy and memorable?

That's it for quotes. We'll take it as read that the quote-gathering process runs in tandem with such other story-making activities as gathering pictures, sound, et cetera. We should also acknowledge that any effective process structured around something as unpredictable as the news can never be expected to be as orderly as, say, the process of drawing up your company's annual report (bet you don't need a whole day to do that). There's always an element of chaos, and anything is welcome whenever it comes. Feel free to offer "sexy" (to use the industry term for eye-catching) pictures and anything else at the time of your interview.

Having gathered at least some of the quotes/sound bites the journalist requires, and having picked up enough knowledge along the way, she will now attempt to write the story (or script the report, or whatever). While trying to concentrate on doing this, she will take incoming phone calls and interruptions from various parties ("We're short of news. Could you make it 800 words rather than 400?") and while ("Are you using any music? There's no music at all so far today.") the interruptions ("Any way you could use a pic of a pig?") continue ("Smith's picture has come in and it's much better than Jones's. Are you using Jones up front?") she will also have to think about ("Sorry, could you run to 1,200 words? We've lost an ad.") a title and an intro, and if this is broadcast ("We've rejigged the running order. You're going first."), she will have to organise ("Sorry, when I said earlier we hadn't got music, we've now got too much music.") any material she didn't think to organise when she had time, equipment and a camera crew to do it properly.

And if it's print ("Make it 1,500 words if you possibly can. But that's too much for one story. Could you break out a couple of boxes?"), she'll also be thinking about pictures. There might be ("Peterson's mugshot has come in and it looks like it was taken in a photo booth. We're sending a photographer. Can you set it up?") a house style dictating the use of ("There's been a military coup in Farawayland. We only need 400 words after all. Sorry.") head-and-shoulders shots, or she might have the opportunity to use ("Sorry, the pig's gone. But we've got a nice pic of a yacht, if you're interested?") something more eye-catching. Similarly, for broadcast, she might suddenly have an inspiration that, let's say, the story would be perfect if she could only find ("That guy you interviewed this morning? He's on the line wondering whether you got everything you needed. Do you want to talk to him?") about ten seconds of footage of cows being milked.

The semi-finished product will pass through an editorial and production process during which ("That guy again? Says he's had second thoughts about the quotes he approved this morning. Could you change 'while' to 'whilst' in the third line of the second quote?") it becomes increasingly difficult to alter – or at least, difficult to alter on the journalist's say-so ("The coup's fizzled out. We need the other 1,000 words and we need it now?"). The only thing worse than interrupting the writing of a story is trying to change a story that's just been put to bed.

If you need it spelled out, here is the conclusion that you should draw from this section:

> Writing/producing a story is a complex process that is already interrupted enough. However, if you've got something good, and you're lucky enough to ring just as the journalist is told she's got another 1,000 words to fill, you'll make a friend for life – or at least, for the rest of this news cycle.

Alternatively, you might like to reflect on how important the little details can suddenly become. You may have given the perfect interview, but if the aftermath was anything like the production process depicted above, your chance of true fame really depended upon whether you thought to mention, perhaps in the lift going down from your office, that you also kept at home a herd of photogenic pet cows.

How does a journalist's memory work?

This is a more serious question than it might seem. First, given the unpredictable but pressured environment in which they work, journalists do remember people who put obstacles in their way. If you waste an interview talking about your company instead of the big issue that interests them, they won't come back. If you mess around with the quotes ("while" to "whilst" is a strangely common correction), they won't want to repeat the experience so they'll be reluctant to interview you again.

But there's a more important question here about the journalistic attention span and what kind of information they want to know, when they want to know it, and how much (and which bits) they will retain.

Three points:

1 Journalists will always remember a worthwhile contact, which they define as a readily available person who speaks in quotes/sound bites (they will also remember somebody who is, in their terms, a time-waster).

2 While they're researching a story, journalists will be keen to listen to anything you have to say about their angle and subject (assuming no time constraints; also, they won't stop you if your idea of relevance is talking about your company non-stop, because you might say something quotable about the subject eventually, but they won't come back for more).

3 Journalists will have forgotten everything you tell them, and some will have forgotten they interviewed you, pretty much as soon as their story has been published or broadcast.

Underlying all of the above is this simple fact:

Journalists do not get involved in the subjects they research.

They don't work in your industry. They've only got so much of their intellect committed to your industry. That commitment will only last until they finish this story and move on to the next.

The skill that a journalist brings to an interview is not his interest (or lack of it) in your subject, nor his interest (or lack of it) in what you have to say. No. A journalist's skill is in drawing out the information he needs, plus quotes, and in absorbing enough know-how to produce a story that gives the impression that it has been written by somebody who knows what he's talking about. Note the use of the word "impression" there. A big part of the skill is also the knack of writing readably about practically anything.

If you're talking to a journalist on a Sunday paper, for example, it's a good bet that this time last week, they were researching an equally lengthy feature on something completely different. You can also bet that they'll be doing something else completely different next week. It has to be different because the readership won't read the same stuff two weeks running.

What does this mean? Simple:

Journalists are professionally required to develop a short attention span.

Speaking from experience (as an interviewee), it is an instructive process to be caught up in a Friday-night crisis on a Sunday newspaper, with the whole resources of the paper concentrated on a late-breaking news story for which you are a key contact, and then to try to get the attention of any of the same people in the following week. They just don't remember.

Journalists are very focused people, but the focus changes with the frequency of the publication on which they're working. If the way they remember seems like a form of selective amnesia, well, that's what it is. They focus on what they need to know, when they need to know it, and the rest is just clutter.

How to deliver the follow-up

By now, this should hardly need saying, so it won't take long to say.

Any follow-up phone call should be brief, and there should be a point to it.

If you're emailing in a picture of yourself, say, include the feature title (or subject) and "PIC" in the email title and if you're emailing to a picture desk, stick in the journalist's name as well. Note that email titles are more likely to be read before deletion than the "Please find enclosed" bit inside. Probably worth telling whoever answers the phone in the editorial office that your pic is on the way. Don't insist on talking to the journalist.

It is good practice to include your name, title (as you would like it to be quoted), company name and a contact number that will get to you (not just the switchboard, if you're going to be out) with anything you send.

If you are sending in a printed picture, disc or other physical material, pack it in such a way that (a) it will get delivered to the journalist even though she's known to be busy and (b) it will be identified and opened when it arrives, rather than just shoved to one side. Be specific. "This is a picture for … " written on the packaging will work better than just putting "Urgent". Everything's "Urgent" these days.

And by the way, don't over-sell; indeed, it's probably best not to say anything about how good a picture is, or how relevant a chart might be. You don't want the journalist to be counting on a "fantastic picture" that turns out to be yet another boring product shot.

So what about pictures?

By email, please.

300dpi or better, please.

And could you make it interesting, please?

It's very easy to produce a picture that shows a man or woman in a suit. It's a head-and-shoulders, the person is smiling, and yeah, okay, you look like the kind of person who would be doing the job you're doing. But you also look like everybody else whose mugshot appears in this issue.

There's absolutely no reason why your mugshot should be used any bigger than anybody else's, even if you have delivered a quote so quotable that it's worth highlighting in bold type under your photograph.

It's not hard to be photographed speaking, or making a point, or standing by a window so you get the light on your face. Nor is it difficult to tip your head forward and bring it up just before the shutter clicks so your face has movement in it.

You could put your hand to your chin (especially if you've got eight chins) or pick up the phone or even stand in front of a microphone, but all that's a tad clichéd. Maybe better to think about standing/sitting at an angle to the camera (turning your head to the lens can flatter you), or possibly looking slightly up or slightly down at it, or just about anything else instead of sitting full-face to the camera and settling into a slightly nervous grin.

If you spend money on promotional literature, think about spending a little on making the people in the company look alive.

If you hire a photographer, hire a news photographer, not somebody who specialises in weddings.

If a title sends a photographer, think about background and think about the many different occasions on which the paper might use the pics they are now going to have on file. Probably best to give them the serious face as well as the smiling face, just in case the news is bad one day.

From one interview to the next

There is one time when you can guarantee that a journalist will not be interested to hear your story. That is immediately after your story has been given comprehensive coverage. Readers/viewers want variety, and journalists are adept at switching from one subject to another, from one edition to the next, from one set of interviewees to the next.

You don't get lucky the same way twice in quick succession. But do remember that any title will have a variety of spaces to fill. A newspaper might have a City Diary as well as a regular in-depth analysis slot, for example, just as the radio doesn't only start the day with the big political interview. There's the business report, the human-interest items, the light relief, the two-people-disagreeing-in-the-interests-of-balance stuff, the various fillers. On Radio 4's *Today* programme, it is not unknown for the occasional management guru to deliver the *Thought For The Day*. Got any thoughts for today?

If you've just been comprehensively "done" by a title, and you see some value in keeping your name in front of the public, think around the different types of coverage that you could get. There's always space for a diary item that's interesting, for example, and if there's any kind of customer analysis that you could pull together into a survey – go for it.

If you're completely out of ideas – read or tune into the title in question. Every time you think, "I could have done that," make a note to be the person who does it next time.

When is a good time to call a journalist?

If you're returning a journalist's call, the best time to do it is now, before she picks up the phone to call somebody else.

Otherwise, the problem is that journalists tend to work a relatively unstructured day. Typically, they start late and work late, although this isn't universal either. Journalists, especially freelance journalists, develop their own individualistic working patterns, with only deadlines (and news conferences for staffers) to provide a structure.

So start your call by asking:

Is this a good time to call? If they say no, **get off the phone**. Don't just say something quickly. **Get off the phone**. It's not that they're in a meeting and they can only spare ten seconds. It's that they're in mid-paragraph and if you don't shut up they're going to lose the thread. Ask when would be a better time, but after that, **get off the phone**. Now.

Although there are no clear guidelines on when to call and not to call, some times are almost certainly better than others.

So here are some guidelines, although note that working practices vary from journalist to journalist and title to title, and can vary according to what's going on in the world, or indeed in the relevant business sector.

It is never a good time to call a news journalist in the immediate aftermath of a major news event. It is always a good time to call a journalist if something big has just happened in your line of business and you can talk authoritatively about it.

Broadcasters, whether radio or television, tend not to be available while their programme is on air.

Nor is it likely that they will welcome a chance to chat in the hour (or two) before the show, nor in the half hour (or more) when they're winding down afterwards.

Daily-newspaper journalists tend to be preoccupied around the end of the day, when they're writing. During the day, it's likely that they will pick up the phone from around 10am, when they get in, to 10.45-ish, which is when they will be starting to think about the morning news conference. You might want to try again before lunch, say from 11.30 to shortly after twelve, and then again after lunch but before the afternoon news conference, so from 2pm-ish to just before 3pm. Then, if you want to start being a nuisance, you can start breaking into their writing-up time from 3.30pm.

You won't get much enthusiasm out of a **weekly** if you call on their press day, but immediately after that, when they're all contemplating the completely blank pages of the next issue, they might be delighted to hear from you (although allow for days off and trips out to the shops). **Sunday papers** tend to be seriously busy from Thursday, but effectively asleep on Mondays; probably best to call on Tuesday or Wednesday.

As for **monthlies**, there will be a period of days, possibly a week, before their official publication date, during which you probably won't get through at all. The issue has cleared to the printers and they're all out to lunch. If you want to hit the news pages, therefore, call at least a week before publication. For features, probably best to give it about six weeks. They're on the case, probably started with their research, but not yet writing.

Online publications, whether stand-alone or tied to an offline title, do not have to contend with the production constraints that dictate the timetables of broadcast and print media. In general, their primary objective is to address the needs of a readership whose behaviour is largely unpredictable, although one increasingly common approach is to time the uploads of new "editions" in advance of peak reader-traffic times. Thus, an online business title might want to publish new content early in the morning, to be available as office-based systems wake up and go online, with updates through the day and particularly before the lunch break and before the evening switch-on time for home-based systems. As a general rule, it is sensible to assume that the online equivalent of an offline title will follow a broadly offline working pattern, while a purely online title will tend to work more as a daily, although with less rigid timing of its news conferences.

And finally … when is a good time to be sitting by the phone?

We've discussed elsewhere how helpful it is to be available post-interview for any last-minute fact-checking. Perhaps it's also worth adding, just briefly, that the likeliest time for facts to need checking is while the story is being written. The previous section may also be read, therefore, as a guide to when to be available. If you've just been interviewed by a daily newspaper, for example, the likeliest time for the phone to ring is around five in the evening.

7

Crisis Management

Introduction

If you've got a crisis breaking right now, skip this introduction and go straight down to the next section. (If you've been misquoted or misrepresented in the media, and that's turning into a crisis, read the section "PR and media crises" below and also refer to Chapter 8.)

This is the chapter in which we discuss the media-handling of sudden, unexpected bad news. By definition, a crisis is something that happens very unexpectedly and remarkably inconveniently. You don't know what it's going to be until it happens, but you do know, first, that it will probably happen at the time when you're least prepared for it, and secondly, that if it isn't handled correctly and efficiently, it will be disastrous for your company (and possibly for you personally, in career terms).

This chapter tries to address crisis management without making any assumption as to what the crisis might be. It could be anything from one customer with food poisoning, to a fire at a warehouse, to a letter in a newspaper or a posting on a blog, to the discovery that a food product contains a banned additive, to the sudden public revelation that, let's say, the personnel director has fled to South America with a bulging suitcase and there's no money in the pension fund. Whatever the crisis, the one thing you know is: it's going public. Now.

All of those crises, and all other possible crises, however large or small, have two characteristics in common. The first is that you need to be ready for them well in advance and you need to stay ready for them. Getting ready might mean drawing up a crisis-management strategy paper and circulating it around key personnel, but it's far more likely to mean getting into the habit of carrying the most important contact numbers with you wherever you go. It's also likely to mean thinking through your own contactability in a crisis. Who has your number? And if a crisis happened, would anybody think to call you?

That second question gets important where, for example, the crisis happens while you're at your daughter's wedding, or on holiday, or where it happens in a department run by somebody who, let's say, likes to run things pretty much independently of the rest of the company. You might be the chief executive. You might be the communications director. You might just be the company's most prominent "media guy", in that you're the one who's always talking to the media, but whoever you are, wherever you are, can you be sure that the people on the spot will call you in a crisis?

Perhaps you should put out that strategy paper after all. Establish a loose definition of a crisis (loose, because you don't want anybody deciding that any given bad news doesn't quite fit the definition, so can be ignored), and make it clear that if bad things happen, you'd rather know than not know. (And make sure your staff understand that they can call you at 4am without fear of criticism if the crisis blows over after all.)

When you're preparing for a crisis, there are two things you need to do. They are:

1   Make sure that when a crisis happens, you will find out about it straight away.

2   Make sure that when a crisis happens, you will be able to alert the key people straight away.

There's something else, too. When a crisis hits, you need to ensure open lines of communication and a rapid, uninhibited exchange of information. This should go through you to the outside world, but it should also go to anybody else in the organisation who might be approached by the media. You don't want people refusing to comment (except as discussed later in this chapter), but you do want them referring enquiries to you for a fuller answer. Put that in your strategy paper too.

The second characteristic that all crises have in common is this:

They need to be handled.

This chapter will focus on the media-management of crises. But remember throughout that you have to deal with the crisis first, and the media impact of the crisis second. Any variant on the line, "I called the media before I called the emergency services" will go down badly. You don't have to know everything that's being done before you can speak to the media, but you do have to know that it is being done.

If you think that a lot of crisis management is actually information management, you're right. The real skills here are getting the information, and keeping it moving.

So. A crisis happens. Are you the first to know? How long before you know? Who else knows? Who are you going to tell? When?

Now read on.

Covered in this chapter:

- The first three rules of crisis management

- What if the media don't know yet?

- Information overload good, speculation bad

- The trust issue

- Internal opposition

- Internal communications

- Relationship management

- The counter-story

- Your competitor's crisis

- How to leak

- Blame and responsibility

- Dealing with negative spin

- PR and media crises

- Blogs

- Letters to the editor

- When a crisis goes bad

- How to say "No Comment"

- The non-answer

- The non-denial denial

- How to stop talking

- The "Fuck Strategy"

- Telling lies

- Case studies

- And finally … what if it's only a small crisis?

The first three rules of crisis management

The first three rules of crisis management are:

1   Get your story in first.

2   Tell it yourself.

3   Tell it all.

Here's another one.

Check the facts. Don't go public with anything that isn't a certainty. In a recent mining disaster, relatives were told that the miners had survived. Then, hours later, they were told that the miners had all died. In fact, they had been dead at the time of the first announcement. To be responsible for such a mistake would be a heavy burden.

Three more rules are:

5   Update the story as frequently as you can.

6   When you don't know something, say so.

7   Be available.

This isn't just a matter of being generous to the news organisations. Because it's a crisis, and by definition out of your control, they're going to report the story anyway. Therefore, they're going to be looking for sources of information. You want to be their primary source.

So here goes.

If you're looking at a major crisis that's breaking now, call the most influential journalist you know. Come clean. Tell the story. Not just your side. The whole story. What you know and what you don't know. Get your team working the phones to call all the other journalists you/they know. Circulate your home number to as many journalists as you can reach.

Don't deny. Don't explain. The priority now is to make yourself the primary source for the *facts* of the situation.

Everybody involved, you included, will have a spin. Don't have journalists requesting facts from people whose spin will be negative. And *don't* try to put a positive spin on the situation, because if you do, they might look to the negative side for balance.

Done all that? Now find out everything you can about the crisis. Set up information feeds so that, first, you get to know everything as soon as it happens, and secondly, you get to update journalists as frequently as you can.

In any spare time you might have, compile background briefings (delegate some of this) on, for example, the working of the component that failed, the chemical composition of the product that's just poisoned all your customers, maps of the refinery that blew up, et cetera. The objective here is to fill up the feature pages. As the newspapers block out the follow-up stories on pages 3, 4, 5, 6, 7 and the Comment page, you will want to remain their primary source.

Television will need some new pictures. Give them some. Send out some eminent professors or people in white coats who can stand in front of diagrams explaining what happened. Show television crews round a production site like the one that blew up. Get your favourite reporters in helicopters flying over the sea where the tanker went down.

There is a crisis-management timetable whereby a crisis matures, in print terms, from the front page to the feature pages and then on until it dies finally in a news round-up somewhere below the fold on page 18. It then rises from the grave when the official enquiry produces its report, or the case comes to court.

Your job is to hand-hold the media throughout, but to adjust the information you're supplying, from news updates to in-depth stuff for the features to a statement welcoming the official report. No two crises are the same in their timetables, but if yours looks like staying on the news agenda for a while, be aware of the need to vary the information feed. If journalists want to keep a story alive, they'll keep it alive. But after a while, they'll start wanting different information. Let them get it from you.

And spend money. If a crisis threatens the company's survival, there's not a lot of point in holding budget meetings about how much to spend on it. And any hint that you're limiting spending will give a very bad impression. Of course you can afford accommodation for the innocent bystanders whose homes were demolished by the runaway bulldozer.

Above all, keep up the dialogue. The underlying message of, "Let me tell you the facts," is, "Let me be honest with you." Put out whatever quantity of information is necessary to keep the initiative. You want to be the one acting - putting out the news - rather than the one reacting. Once you lose the initiative, so that the media are coming to you for your reaction to somebody else's version of events, you begin to look as though you're correcting, denying, explaining, catching up. Potentially, you make yourself vulnerable to being portrayed as the bad guy.

What if the media don't know yet?

If the crisis hasn't yet gone public, you have a decision to make. If it is certain to go public eventually, you may judge that your best move is to alert the media. The argument in favour of doing this is that you will immediately make yourself the primary source of information on the crisis. The argument against going public is … difficult to sustain, if you're clear that the story is going to break sooner or later.

Never, ever, allow yourself to think in terms of covering up a crisis.

Information overload good, speculation bad

There are some limits to this barrage of information, of course. If the crisis is just that the managing director ran over a pensioner's cat, you probably don't need the helicopters flying over the scene. But there is an important principle here:

> In any crisis, it is always better to over-supply information than to under-supply it. No journalist should ever be short of a fact or short of a source of a fact.

Notice that we're talking about information and facts. Avoid speculation. Restrict yourself to the facts. If you're invited to speculate on blame, or liability, say, "I don't know" (and see below). If they persist, eventually hand out the contact details of the company's lawyers. You can't do better than that.

And don't blame anybody else (also see below). If there's a consensus developing that the duty maintenance crew should not have gone out drinking that night, don't fall into the trap of agreeing that they might be to blame for the loss of the refinery. There will, of course, be an enquiry, and you can't prejudge the results of the enquiry. Right now, the company's primary concern is to ensure safety, et cetera. Stay on the narrow path of handing out information.

The trust issue

In a crisis, trust is fragile. It is possible for a trusted spokesperson to emerge in a crisis, and have an influence on the outcome, but this status must be protected. Do not try to guide the story, or in any way tell the media how to cover it. Be frank, and if necessary, be frank about your ignorance. Most important of all, don't be evasive, and don't lie. If you're evasive, you're the bad guy.

Internal opposition

The two biggest problems you're likely to face when you set out to manage a crisis will come from inside your organisation.

The first is that various groups within the organisation will want to hold meetings about the crisis before they go public with any information. It may be that the managing director wants to get the board together to discuss the situation before deciding what to do. It may be that there is a big question over legal liability, say, or that your insurers require notification before authorising any expenditure. It may be simply that there's a turf war between two directors over whose responsibility it is to react to the crisis.

A crisis, by definition, is outside your control. While your people are debating the situation, the news media are being contacted by, say, customer groups, contact groups, pressure groups, cranks, former employees who once worked in the refinery that blew up, freelance "experts" who can describe what might have happened, and any number of independent commentators on your industry.

The doomsday scenario is where your company becomes paralysed in the aftermath of a crisis. Inside, everybody is talking, but every time they get something together on which to go public, the story changes before they can get it out. So they have another meeting.

It is very difficult to provide advice for such a situation, except to say that (a) any good crisis management strategy should establish, in the large print, in advance, with everybody's agreement, the need for immediate issuance of facts, and (b) that sometimes, it's conceivable that there might just possibly be a case for reacting to a crisis before you're told not to react to it yet. Your call.

The second big internal problem may turn out to have been the cause of the first. Organisations can make the mistake of thinking that because there's something called "crisis management", crises can be managed into a more favourable shape. This is a mistake. You cannot manage a crisis into becoming something other than a crisis. Nor will a crisis sit still while you hold meetings to find ways of making it go away.

Again, it's difficult to offer advice for dealing with this situation, except to say that crisis management requires a degree of autonomy. If you work in a company with rigid reporting structures and a very clearly defined hierarchy, well, think about it. You might also want to read the sections later in this chapter on what to do when a crisis turns bad.

For now, here's the rule:

> You can't make a bad situation good. The objective of crisis management should be to make the impact of a bad situation less negative.

Sorry, but you've got to own up.

Internal communications

In a crisis, your staff also need to know what is going on. If it's a major crisis, they also need to know that they might get calls from the media. It is a good idea to ensure, first, that an effective system of internal communication is in place, and secondly, that staff are aware that they should refer media enquiries to your office. In some crises, staff Q&A sessions have been held to good effect.

Relationship management

Here, at last, is where you learn how important it is to have relationships with the key journalists in your industry. We have discussed relationship-building already (see Chapter 2), and if you have taken the trouble to get to know the key people on the key titles, working with them through bad times as well as good, giving interviews on industry issues even when there's nothing in it for you, this is the time when you'll reap the benefit.

Think about it. If you're a total stranger to the person behind the microphone, you're going to have to start the interview facing whatever set of preconceptions they've built up from the situation around them. Given that this is a bad situation, their thoughts might be negative before you even start.

But if you're dealing with somebody who already knows that you're friendly, talkative, human, et cetera, you'll be starting with an edge.

Look around you. Who are the journalists you'd really need on your side in a crisis? Could you get to know them better?

The counter-story

It is tempting, but dangerous, to attempt to put out a counter-story in a crisis situation. Your chemical factories might be leaking poison into the atmosphere, but at least your green-fuel lab has come up with an idea for steam-driven cars. Your equity fund might have collapsed, but at least your bond fund is doing well.

This tactic almost always turns out badly. It amounts to a form of evasion. Don't do it. You can continue with any scheduled sequence of news releases if you must (some stories just won't work post-crisis), but trying to get everybody to look the other way should not form part of your crisis-management strategy.

If a larger crisis elsewhere deflects attention from your own crisis, do not change your crisis-management strategy. The pressure may be off, but you don't want to be caught relaxing. If you are asked about the other crisis, express sympathy, if appropriate offer support, but stay focused. And note this:

There is no competition in crisis management. (See below.)

Do not attempt to release bad news in the wake of a major (inter)national crisis that might deflect attention from your organisation. In the wake of the 9/11 tragedy, a young civil servant circulated the suggestion to her UK government department that this might be "a good time to bury bad news". Much of the coverage of this deplorable suggestion names organisations that did release bad news post-9/11, whether deliberately or because the news (results, etc.) had to go out then for legal reasons.

Your competitor's crisis

If your competitor suffers a crisis, you can either offer support or stay out of it. Do not ever seek to gain competitive advantage from a crisis. You may gain some degree of goodwill from offering, let's say, your company's fire trucks to put out their fire, but your objective should be to put out the fire rather than to get the goodwill.

Also, if you might be tempted to offer limited help, think through the potential downside. In an insurance crisis, you might offer to take on the crisis-hit company's policies, let's say. But if you limit that offer to young, non-smoking, virtually risk-free policy-holders, don't expect to win friends in the media.

How to leak

Sometimes, there may be information that you can't release, that would help the situation along. It might be that, for example, the media aren't looking in the right place, or they keep on getting some aspect of the story wrong, or that if only they knew – something – they'd understand.

Take a lot of care here. All journalists like to get something that nobody else has got. No journalist is entirely reliable with a leak, not least because sometimes, their sources make the mistake of leaking something that could only have come from one or two places.

Leaking information deliberately also looks like leaking information deliberately. Everybody records everything, and if you go to a journalist with a story or an angle that's been missed, you're putting a dent in your role as the person who's putting out the facts, all the facts, and nothing but the facts.

Don't leak information. It's not your job in this crisis.

If you are going to leak, don't do it directly. That might mean making an indirect reference to something and letting the journalist work out the rest of it, or it might mean that your PR person might let something slip. You might even do the thing they do in the movies, leaving a file open on your desk while you slip out to get a coffee.

If you are going to leak, only ever do it to a journalist you trust. Never to a group of journalists. Never after a drink. And never on the spur of the moment.

Blame and responsibility

Never blame another person or another organisation. Shifting blame, however justifiably, looks bad. This is partly because your main focus is supposed to be on sorting out the crisis rather than getting out from under it.

There will come a time when the main fires have been put out and you're invited to agree with various statements on whose fault it all was. This is a dangerous time. For a whole range of reasons, mostly legal, you may not be able to admit responsibility. That's fine. But don't park it somewhere else either. Again, there are legal considerations, but the main media-handling priority is to avoid having your name used alongside the word "deny" as in "denied responsibility". Better, you might say, not to prejudge the results of the enquiry, or the internal investigation, or whatever, which you will of course promise to release in full when it comes.

Responsibility is a bigger word than blame, and more complex to handle. You are accepting responsibility for handling the crisis. You have taken over. As to responsibility for causing the crisis, it's not so much that you're not willing to answer the question, as that you don't have the facts on which to give a full answer. You'll be happy to answer that question, but you can't prejudge the results, et cetera.

Never suggest that another person or another organisation is responsible. If you start doing that, you demonstrate your willingness to prejudge, et cetera.

Dealing with negative spin

This is a crisis, right? A bad thing has happened and you're fielding the bad impact on your company. You are not fighting for a happy ending but for a less-unhappy ending and the chance of a new beginning.

Remember that when you get hit by negative spin. There will be people and organisations who don't want you to succeed. They might be disaffected customers, or if you're a big company with a big crisis to handle, (inter)national organisations with an agenda of their own.

So your crisis happens. You do everything right and get to be the media's main source of information. Then some pressure group, or disaffected customer, calls up a TV channel (or issues a press release to everybody) offering interviews to state the case that your crisis was inevitable because your company has lax safety standards, an accident waiting to happen, typical of a company that's so incompetent that it can't – whatever. There's always something and it always sounds quite convincing.

- Don't get mad.

- Forget about getting even.

- Don't retaliate.

- Don't point out the obvious (to you) fact that this person is a loon (although, come to think of it, there can be times when it's a good move to check through the customer-correspondence files).

Unfortunately, negative spin works for the media in a crisis situation. Whatever its merits, it's another side to the story. It's a new angle. It's a fresh set of quotes and a new mugshot. It's a box they can put on page one with "Full story – page three" at the end. The broadcast presenters get to practise their concerned voices.

And, frankly, there's an audience for negative stuff. This gets their attention and thus expands the overall audience.

The danger of spin is that it tempts you into a head-to-head fight. You won't win it. Even if you're right, you won't win it. This is because, at a time like this, you lose by being seen to get into a fight.

Stay focused on the crisis. Don't get side-tracked. The logic of your position is that you can't afford to get into a squabble right now.

Keep going with the information and the updates. If you have to respond, and it can look robotic not to sometimes, you will come out better saying quotably that you have a good track record on safety, for example, than if you're quoted rubbishing the other guy for not knowing anything about safety.

There can be circumstances where you would welcome the input from the pressure group, if they'd like to call you, and of course, if your dissatisfied customer would like to get in touch, you'll happily set him straight.

But don't think about beating the negative spin with positive spin. Think about continuing to be heard. It's a distraction, it's unwelcome, it's (not always) unjustified and it may be unfair.

But you're not in this to win. You're in it to lose by a smaller margin.

PR and media crises

You might have been misquoted, misrepresented or otherwise badly treated by the media. It may be that this treatment is having a negative effect on, say, the sales of a product or the share price of the company.

The successful outcome of this crisis will require, first, a public acknowledgement that your product is not as bad as the original coverage suggested, and secondly, a memo to all sales people and other staff drawing their attention to the new positive coverage. It might also require payment of damages, et cetera, but we're not going to talk about that here.

Chapter 8 takes you through the legalities. The purpose of this brief section is to persuade you that, in a media crisis of this kind, you may be more successful if you negotiate a settlement than if you shout down the phone and call in the lawyers.

First step, be calm. Second step, set a priority. You want publicity in the form of a friendlier set of press cuttings and/or recordings and you also want to preserve your long-term relationship with the journalist(s) and/or title(s) involved. This is not to suggest that if you go to law, your favourite newspaper will never speak to you again, but the general principle is: if you can find a friendly way out of a crisis like this, take it.

Third step, ask yourself whether your relationship(s) with the journalist(s) and editor(s) involved are strong enough for you to handle this yourself, and whether in any case you might prefer to involve your PR people. There are advantages to involving your own team of "pre-legal" third parties in this kind of crisis, not least in that a PR person could spread the news of a resolution to other titles.

There are three primary explanations for negative coverage:

1 It was a mistake.
2 They believe it to be true (and would argue justification).
3 There's malice involved.

If the original coverage was a mistake and you can demonstrate this, it is likely that an editor would want to make amends. There has been a movement in recent years for print titles (and to a lesser extent the broadcast media) to highlight corrections as an indirect demonstration of their concern for accuracy. That would do the trick, of course, but don't be hasty. Could you treat this as a relationship-enhancing opportunity? You (or your PR person) might want to suggest, for example, that a better solution might be the opportunity to put your case prominently in a forthcoming feature on the subject? Perhaps you could accept the correction and then have enough of a chat about the feature to enable you to call the journalist writing it if she doesn't call you first? Look for that opportunity.

If they believe the original coverage to have been true, you will have to demonstrate that it wasn't. If you can do this, another relationship-enhancing opportunity suddenly appears, even bigger than the first. Don't blow it. Don't ask them to run a full-page ad for your company on page one, for example. Don't try to get them to sell for you. But there will almost certainly be something you can work out together.

If there's malice involved, keep calm. How high does it go? Start by working out your demonstration that the coverage was wrong and unjustified. If the journalist was against you, take it to the editor. Let the editor draw his own conclusions about the journalist from the facts; it may be that there's an opportunity even here.

But if the whole programme was deliberately hostile or the attack had the whole paper behind it (and even better, if you weren't offered a chance to put your side), the chances are that they won't be receptive to a cosy fireside chat. The chances are that they will be able to support their damaging assertions, at least in the sense that the facts will have been researched and (for example) the aggrieved customers will be genuine, even though the slant they've put on everything is just plain nasty.

How big is the damage? If it is very big, you will have to call in the lawyers, issue a detailed rebuttal, write to customers and staff, cancel all your advertising with that paper or channel, turn to Chapter 8, get into big-time crisis management.

But before you do, consider these two points.

1 If you over-react, you risk publicising the original attack to people who never came across it.

2 Nobody believes journalists, or at least, nobody takes them as seriously as you might have been taking them since this crisis started.

That second point is particularly true where the malicious title is one that specialises in finding a "bad guy" every Sunday for page nine, or every Tuesday for broadcast at 9pm. Perhaps some of them are bad, but can you remember which company it was a month ago? Particularly if other titles aren't picking up the story, do pause to consider how high-profile your response needs to be. Sometimes, you might be better off circulating your rebuttal to customers and staff, quietly briefing key journalists on other titles (perhaps organising a press event), offering to help any genuinely aggrieved customers you can identify, and then letting the whole thing be forgotten.

Blogs

Blogs, or "web logs", fit under the crisis-management heading because a hostile mention in a blog has all the characteristics of a crisis. It's sudden, unexpected, potentially damaging and outside your control. A complicating factor is that any blog will typically appeal to a special-interest group, whether the special interest is politics, Zen Buddhism, hairdressing or grappling with the complexities of your company's products (enter 'blog' and 'product' into Google for examples of this type of blog). Special-interest groups tend to feel their grievances more strongly than the rest of us.

A further complicating factor is that bloggers link to each other, so that the complaint about your product can be spread to a wider audience quickly (the 'comment' facility on a blog can also attract 'me-too' complainants). Bloggers are typically not trained and/or experienced journalists with an instinct for accuracy and/or truth, and although this does not necessarily mean that you are uniquely vulnerable to biased and inaccurate reporting with blogs, it doesn't mean anything else either.

Practical responses to an adverse mention on a blog might include the following.

- **Do nothing immediately**. This is the only place in this chapter where you will find this suggestion. A hostile blog gains a lot from being taken seriously by the company concerned. Do not show that you take it seriously.

- **Take it seriously**. This is a disaffected customer speaking. Can you help? If you can 'turn' a disaffected customer, maybe you'll get some positive feedback. (Remember, however, that refunding a blogger might trigger claims from his audience!) The other reason to take a blog seriously is the potential size of its audience, its accessibility and the speed with which the complaint can be duplicated.

- **When/if you do respond, do so via the blog**. Whatever other eruptions might be occurring in the company - denials, sackings, product recalls, meetings with lawyers - make it personal and make yourself small. "I'm the person at the company who launched that product, and I'm sorry you're having trouble with it," comes across better than an injunction against repeating the complaint (which will of course be picked up by other blogs). By putting your response on the blog, you ensure that it is seen by the people most likely and best equipped to take the matter further.

- **Keep it small and close it down**. If you manufacture cars that are exploding because you put the fuel tank next to the cigarette lighter, this is going to be big. But if it's just one disaffected individual, address it at that level. The 'blogosphere' is not a business environment in which sledgehammers are effective tools for cracking nuts (see also 'Dealing with members of the public' in Chapter 4).

Letters to the editor

If a customer of your company writes a letter to the editor of a print publication to complain about you, perhaps in response to a story in which you were quoted, and it's published, do two things:

1 Solve the customer's problem directly.

2 Write a letter to the editor giving a response to the criticism and including the news that you have dealt directly with the customer. Don't say, but let it be assumed, that your customer is now happy.

If your letter was not published in the next issue, you would have grounds for complaint. However, this is an unusual situation. Any reader is a direct customer of a publication, and may expect a credible complaint to be taken up by the publication (if it's not ignored). There is a proliferation of columnists taking on big companies on behalf of individual readers, not least because the resulting columns are personal, specific, depict situations with which other readers can identify, and make the publication look good.

If a print title did pick up your customer's letter, therefore, you could expect to be contacted by the title's "consumer champion", who might even write under that title or another like it. This person should be taken seriously.

If your customer had contacted a broadcast consumer-affairs programme, the same would happen. From here on, this section applies equally to broadcast and print media.

The first snag is that customers don't make their first complaint to the media. You will find, therefore, that your customer not only has a problem, but has a problem that your company has already failed to resolve.

Find out very quickly indeed what the customer's problem was, whether it was genuine, so that this complaint is justified, and what happened to it. If the problem was genuine, solve it. Now. Then list all the failures in your procedures and do something about them. You are going to have to own up to this lot, so you'd better be able to say that you've sorted them out.

If the customer's problem wasn't genuine, you should be sympathetic, understanding, nice about it, et cetera. It has become the consumer champion's story now, and you can't tell a journalist to drop a story. Let the champ make that decision.

If it's Friday and the column's due to run on Sunday, you may end up getting a column on your efficient customer-handling system.

If the customer's problem was genuine, your message for the interview is:

- You've sorted it out.

- You've uncovered a small number of similar cases and sorted them out too.

- What went wrong in your system was [assuming you can point to some reasonable flaw, be specific about it; otherwise, talk about misunderstandings, failures of communication, et cetera]. Do avoid any explanation that could be interpreted as, say, we've got so many customers, our systems can't keep up.

- You're committed to a high standard of customer service (this is the one interview in which they might actually quote you saying that).

- We pride ourselves on being very responsive to our customers' needs (ditto).

Whether or not the customer's problem was genuine, you should not:

- Seek to minimise the issue. The consumer champion's judgement was: this is worth chasing. Don't attack that judgement.

- Be evasive. Ever. But particularly not now.

- Seek in any way to get the journalist on your side against the customer, or criticise the customer to the journalist.

One final thought. A customer who complains to one title might complain to two. If you are contacted by two titles about the same customer's problem, there's no harm in mentioning each to the other. If you're really lucky, both might drop it.

When a crisis goes bad

It is in the nature of any crisis-management operation that the situation can get worse. The negative spin continues. The media begin to turn against you. Crucial information emerges that you couldn't have released earlier because you didn't know it. A regulator suddenly announces an independent enquiry.

A crisis can also go bad because you reach a stage at which there are things you just can't say. The lawyers are involved, perhaps, and the crisis has matured to the point at which every other question is about blame and responsibility.

When a crisis goes bad, the other thing that happens is that people panic. This can make them act irrationally. Sometimes, they even start to brief against you. However they do it, whether or not deliberately, your colleagues can make it difficult for you to keep the show on the road.

You have several options:

- The first is to continue with crisis-management. If you're going to do this, the only option is to continue as before. There is no alternative method that will work as well.

- However, you may find it necessary to develop a strategy of referring questions upwards, or sideways. If you're lucky, the lawyers will tell you to shut up.

- Another option is to discontinue your crisis-management operation. This may be difficult to do, because the media don't just let go, and you may judge it necessary to leak (see above) your true feelings about the situation to a trusted journalist.

- Another option is to resign.

As a crisis deteriorates, you will find that the interviews get tougher, the press conferences more difficult. The following sections suggest some techniques you might have to use if the endgame is not going your way.

How to say "No Comment"

Here is how to say, "No Comment".

You open your mouth and say, "No Comment". Nothing else. You can smile if you like, but don't say anything like, "I'm not going to answer that question." If you're asked, "Why won't you comment?" the correct answer is, "No Comment". The correct answer to, "People are going to draw their own conclusions from your silence," is, wait for it, "No Comment".

"No Comment" is as close as you can get to silence without staying silent. The phrase also indicates that you're ready for the next question. "No Comment" is the only form of words that actually means "No Comment". Anything else is easier to challenge than "No Comment". But you have to stick to it.

The non-answer

You're on television. Probably live. Somebody asks you a really awful question that you really don't want to answer. What do you do?

You don't deal with the question directly. You don't waffle. You don't go red and say "Er" a lot.

You learn forward in your chair, looking serious. You give them an answer. Not to the question they've asked, but to a question like it that works better for you. As you're doing it, you continue to look like somebody who's answering a serious question. If you like, you can use phrases like, "I think the real issue here is … " Make the answer longer than your answers usually are. Use up their time.

They can only use a sound bite you give them.

The audience will draw conclusions from your tone of voice.

The interviewer will know what you're doing, and if you're unlucky, she will try the question again. Same trick, slightly different answer. If you're lucky, she'll run out of time. Then, when they're looking for sound bites for the 30-second slot they've got booked on the late news, they'll be stuck with you saying something confident.

The non-denial denial

This is a political trick. Politicians use it a lot. It's a method of not telling the truth that isn't quite lying. In politics, there may (or may not) be occasions on which its use is justified. In business, don't use it unless you're in real trouble and there's no better way out. (Also, never get into a situation where you might have to use it.)

The non-denial denial works like this. You're asked, "Did you do it?" You answer, "That's an outrageous suggestion." If they find out later that you did it, you can't be accused of lying because you never actually said that you didn't do it. You just offered the opinion that the suggestion was outrageous.

How to stop talking

We'll assume that you're in an interview that's going badly. Very badly. You're being asked leading questions, and you've already been led half-way to somewhere you really don't want to go. The tape recorder's on, the journalist's notepad is filling up, and you can see the little red light on the camera.

This is a complete disaster, right? There's no way you're going to be able to turn it to your advantage. You're fighting on the interviewer's territory, where she feels at home and you're under the lights. The one thing you know is, if this goes on, the situation is going to get worse.

Stop talking. This is difficult because it breaks the social/psychological rapport that exists between any two people in conversation. But you've got to do it. Stop talking.

The journalist, of course, will be on a roll. She'll behave like anybody would if you stopped dead in mid-conversation.

You could say, "No Comment". But why not give them something they can use?

Say, "Thank you very much." Pause so that there's a time-consuming gap between the last question and what you do now. Unclip the little microphone. Stand up. Leave the studio.

Do it calmly. Don't hurry. Don't say anything. Don't punch the sound man. Don't try to block the camera with your fist. Just go.

The "Fuck Strategy"

This is for emergency use only. If you're giving a recorded interview, for radio or TV, and you realise in mid-sentence that you're saying absolutely the wrong thing, swear. They can't use a sound bite that comprises subject, verb, swear-word, not least because it isn't a complete sentence.

But be sure you're not live. There is an out-take that gets an airing occasionally, in which a senior cabinet minister, realising he's going off-message, says, "Ah, fuck, can we do that again?" Only to be told, "No minister, we're live."

It may be that a live broadcast goes out with a seven-second delay to give time for a "bleep" to be inserted over any unbroadcastable words. First, don't count on this. Secondly, you don't want to go on record saying, "Our product is a bleeping bleep!"

Telling lies

Don't. Lies follow you around. You can go from job to job, even country to country, and still there's the fact on record that you lied. Newspaper columns may disintegrate and digital storage may decay, but you can bet that somewhere, somebody will remember.

Another snag with lying is that it goads whistle-blowers. Somewhere in your organisation is somebody who knows the truth. If they hear it being denied, they will be more likely to want it told.

And by the way, this section is not being written in the belief that any of us would seriously consider lying as a viable crisis-management technique. But if you're going to be facing hostile questioning, it is wise to have decided in advance that you'll say "No Comment" (see above) before you stumble into saying things that you don't want to say.

Case studies

Some real-life crises are easier to discuss than others, so for reasons of taste, decency and aversion to letters from lawyers, this section does not name all the names in all the cases. But there are useful lessons to be learned from how crises have been managed in the past.

Perrier

The best-known crisis-management case study is Perrier. In 1990, the company's management woke up to the news that traces of benzene had been found in bottles of its mineral water. Perrier went public in a big way, recalling and destroying 40 million bottles of water, at a cost of some £20 million, and publicising every move the company made. Result: we're still drinking Perrier.

Exxon

The Perrier story is generally contrasted with the 1989 Exxon Valdez oil spill, during which Exxon limited its communication with the media, and in effect, left the media to take the story from other sources. Result: negative coverage. These two cases underline the principle that it's imperative to keep communicating through a crisis. Keep the media's attention.

Eurotunnel

But it's not that simple. Here is a verbatim transcript of a journalist's recollection of the 1996 Eurotunnel fire:

> *"The fire broke out and the company went straight into crisis-management mode. Regular briefings to the press, everything going well, emergency procedures working out fine. Then the drivers got out of the tunnel. They'd been choking in the smoke and were desperate to escape. When the press latched on to them, it wasn't fine at all."*

US miners

In a more recent tragic case in the US, mentioned earlier, a group of miners became trapped underground. The company issued a statement that the miners were safe shortly before the news emerged that they had all died underground.

Communicate, but never exceed what you know. Always admit ignorance.

Life assurers and their pigeons

In the world of business, another rule might be:

Have good ideas, but don't be too clever.

Way back in the mid-nineties, a Scottish life assurance company had the bright idea of sending pigeons, in boxes, to a number of financial journalists. The birds were all safely packaged, and the idea was that their arrival (and release by the journalists) would be a novel way of highlighting the company's high-flying new initiative. Result: a small number of diary columns posing the questions, what if the boxed pigeons had been delivered a few days late, and what if the journalists hadn't been there to receive and release them?

Ladies' underwear

There's also that case study used on marketing courses, where a manufacturer of ladies' underwear received a letter from a customer complaining that she'd attempted to dry a pair of tights in front of a fire and they'd shrivelled up in the heat. The company wrote back saying, in effect: of course they did, you idiot. Result: sales dried up in that region as all the offended customer's friends switched to another brand. Don't underestimate customers and members of the public.

Access, ignorance and detail

It should go without saying that if you're going to invite the chairman to address a group of journalists at a product launch, you should first ensure that the chairman is on message with such details as the name and key features of the product you're launching. Oh, and make sure there's somebody to unlock the room before everybody arrives. It should also go without saying that if you're delivering journalists to an airport after a successful press trip, you shouldn't leave them until you've made absolutely sure that your people booked as many seats on the flight as you're delivering journalists.

But this section wouldn't be complete without mention of the radio business programme that went out live while its much-trailed star guest listened from reception, having been refused access to the building because somebody forgot to send the necessary memo. Nor of the journalist who recorded a series of interviews and then misquoted everybody because he wrote their names down in the wrong order.

Crisis management is all about communication; crisis avoidance is often about attention to detail.

And finally … what if it's only a small crisis?

There's no such thing. If you define a crisis as something that's gone wrong in public, you would also do well to recognise that every crisis, however apparently small, is big enough to need management.

The snag with a crisis is that unless you manage it effectively, it grows. Even if your crisis is just a single customer complaining of a stomach upset after eating your brand of breakfast cereal, you should work on the assumption that the customer in question has a lot of friends, most of them journalists, all of whom take his advice on what cereal to buy.

8

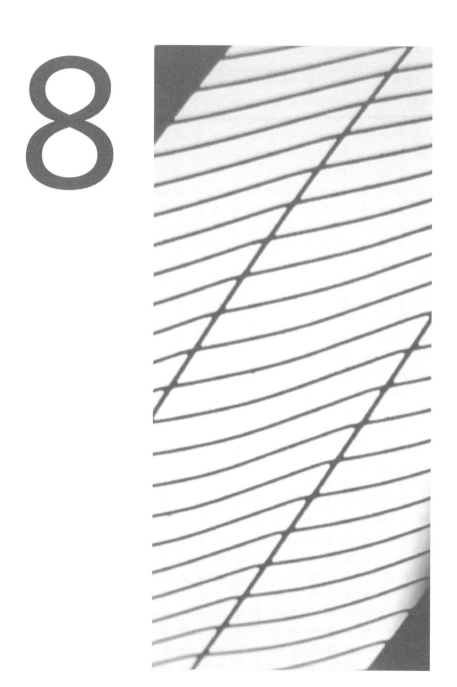

Your Legal Rights
And What To Do With Them

Introduction

This is an entire chapter about something you should try very hard to avoid discovering. Handling the media is a relationship business, and relationships tend to be more easily maintained between people who are *not* addressing each other through their legal representatives. Also, in the context of most business media, the likelihood is that disagreements will be based on misunderstanding, misquotation, inadvertent misrepresentation and at worst inappropriate disclosure of sensitive information, rather than on malice or deliberate falsehood.

At the tabloid end of the media, there is a market for long-lens photographs of undressed celebrities in marital difficulties. On the business/financial pages, the market is different. Although the key imperative is still to fill empty space with interesting information in a hurry, there is also a market for accuracy. If the FT was consistently wrong about the facts, you wouldn't buy it. The latest divorce rumours about a celebrity don't have to be accurate to sell newspapers, but the market reports do. Unfortunately, the "divorce" end of the market colours public perceptions of all the media.

None of the above is intended to suggest that if you are misquoted, or otherwise misrepresented, you should ignore it. Journalists do get things wrong, sometimes deliberately (or at least, knowingly), and a healthy relationship is one in which they know they can't get away with that kind of thing. They also expect their mistakes to be corrected, and a number of titles publish (usually) short columns detailing the latest corrections.

If you prefer a cynical view, a list of corrections is an effective way of advertising a concern for accuracy.

The point is that there is a broadly established procedure for handling complaints against the media. If the situation is serious, you may want to consult your legal team at the outset. But if we're talking about your average, run-of-the-mill idiocy, like misquoting you to the point where you're saying something you'd never say, or publishing important numbers with too many noughts on the end, you may get a more long-term positive result by complaining within the relationship – at first, anyway.

This chapter does run through your legal rights in relation to the media, but it is primarily intended as a practical guide to the use of those rights. For this reason, the first sections below will attempt to convince you not to send for your lawyers, or shout down the phone, if the media treat you inappropriately.

Covered in this chapter:

- Two FAQs on being misquoted

- Public interest, fair comment

- Malice and misconduct

- How to complain

- Your legal rights and theirs

- The Press Complaints Commission (PCC)'s code of practice

- Ofcom's code of practice

- More on recording devices

- Jigsaw identification

- What is an injunction?

- And finally ... useful websites

Two FAQs on being misquoted

Probably the most frequently asked question of all is:

   "What can I do to stop myself being misquoted?"

The second-most frequently asked question is:

   "What can I do if I am misquoted?"

The first question is easy. Cultivate relationships with journalists who, as they come to know you, also come to understand your business. Make sure they have your contact details so that they can check details rather than having to let them go because the deadline has arrived. Speak clearly into their recording devices. Leave as little room for ambiguity as possible. Alternatively, if you think you're likely to be misquoted, don't give the interview.

If you have been misquoted, assess the damage. Is the misquotation likely to do you any harm, and how many of your target audience are likely to believe you said the misquoted version rather than what you really said? Given that you've already gained by being quoted in the first place, what is the net effect of the whole episode? You should call the journalist, but if you make it clear that you're just calling to correct the inaccuracy, rather than to make a fuss, that's a positive.

Public interest, fair comment

Before you complain (other than to correct an inaccuracy or misquotation), ask yourself whether your complaint is valid.

If the coverage at issue could be defended as being in the public interest, it may be that you do not have a defence after all, or that you would have to complain more forcefully and at greater length to be successful, than the situation warrants. While this does not extend to properly confidential or sensitive information, journalists and editors will defend their right to disclose information where disclosure is in the public interest.

If the coverage is an expression of an opinion, ask yourself whether it is fair comment. Everybody, journalists included, has a right to conclude that your product is inferior to a rival's for example. You may have grounds for complaint if the journalist is motivated by malice (see below), but even here, do not complain against the title's right to its opinion.

Where a title publishes fair comment against you, consider other options for retrieving the situation. It may be that you have grounds on which to challenge the negative opinion, in that you can cite product characteristics not mentioned in the original coverage. Consider writing a Letter to the Editor, or offering yourself for interview, and if you do write in, enclose a high-quality picture if possible.

Malice and misconduct

If you are unlucky, you may encounter a journalist who just doesn't like you. The chemistry is wrong between you, or there's some other antagonism that may not be explicable, but that covers any coverage you get from that person.

Avoid. If necessary, complain. But this is difficult territory. A journalist's ability to deal objectively with his contacts is part of his professional skill. An accusation of bias is very serious. Don't end up on the wrong end of the journalist's complaint that you are impugning his professional integrity. If you have to do more than just refuse future interview requests (because this journalist covers your industry for an important title, say), think about complaining to the editor through your PR adviser, and/or think about doing it over a quiet drink rather than in a formal letter.

You have a perfect right to complain to an editor of other forms of misconduct, although the same applies: better to do it informally. One difficulty you might encounter, curiously enough, is identifying misconduct. It is easy enough to spot rudeness, for example, but you should also beware of journalists who seek to take advantage of you.

A travel journalist should not demand the best accommodation on a press trip, for example, any more than, say, a financial journalist should let any "freebie" gifts he receives influence the coverage he provides. There is a fine line between indulging journalists, because they're influential people and you want their goodwill, and letting them take advantage. But increasingly these days, the presumption is that journalists should not even accept goodwill, let alone be influenced by it. Increasingly, editors are on your side in this.

How to complain

As has been implied already, the first step is to decide whether you really need to complain at all. The second is to decide whether you should complain yourself, or leave it to a PR professional who will already have an established relationship with the journalist and/or editor concerned, and who can complain without involving you directly in the complaint.

The third step is to start at the bottom rung of the "ladder of complaint". You may go direct to your lawyers, but even if you do that, and hand the matter over to them, the first step will tend to be an approach to the journalist/editor of the title in question. Note that the editor bears legal responsibility for the published content of the title he edits. On small business titles, it is unlikely that the editor will have the power that should accompany this responsibility, but this is the legal situation. The journalist is personally responsible for content he has produced; the editor is responsible for its publication; generally, this means that both will be joined in any legal action.

Note that if, as is variously suggested earlier in this chapter, you have begun your complaint informally, verbally, without record, it is a distinct second step to put it in writing. You should aim to accumulate a paper trail showing that throughout the complaint process you have been reasonable. Also note that you should keep up a reasonable momentum. It is reasonable to expect a response to a serious complaint within, say, seven days, but you will undermine your own complaint if you're not sufficiently bothered to send a follow-up letter within, say, a fortnight if you haven't heard. And write, don't email.

Conventional advice on complaining is that, at each stage, you should let it be understood that you are prepared to go to the next stage. This applies here. If you are not satisfied with the response of the editor/title itself, set out your complaint in writing and make it clear that you intend now to refer the matter to the Press Complaints Commission (for print) or to Ofcom (for broadcast media). Contact details below and in the "Useful websites" section at the end of this chapter.

At this stage, if you have not done so already, set out what redress you are seeking. This should be proportionate. If you have been libelled, there may be scope for a published apology and payment of substantial damages. If you have been misquoted in a small-circulation trade magazine – no. But if you would be prepared to accept some form of published retraction, perhaps in the form of an apology and then a follow-up article in which the correct situation is made clear, you may be more immediately successful than if you're asking for cash.

Remember that journalists *do* want to fill space and *don't* want to get bogged down in extraneous paperwork. Publishing another article on the same subject, which they'd do anyway sooner or later, would be relatively easy. Having you lined up in advance as a contact, rather than having to go through the process of finding a contact, works as well.

If none of the above resolves your complaint to your satisfaction, your next step is to contact the Press Complaints Commission at www.pcc.org.uk for print media or Ofcom at www.ofcom.org.uk for broadcast. If you are complaining to the BBC, there is an intermediate stage. After the BBC itself, you should refer your complaint to the BBC Governors at www.bbcgovernors.co.uk.

You may find it useful to know that the BBC sets out how it likes to receive complaints at www.bbc.co.uk/complaints. Nothing said there affects your right to complain in your own way, but that address does provide useful links.

Note also that some media companies operate complaints-handling departments. If your letter is identifiably a complaint, it might be routed directly to one of these. But the problem is, such departments don't have the clout to negotiate, say, inclusion in future coverage. This might be another argument for the direct-but-informal approach to the editorial people.

Your legal rights and theirs

You have a right to privacy. The media have a right to free speech. Some journalists would add that the public have a right to know. This is not a precise statement of a set of legal principles, but a brief summary of the big problem at the heart of this chapter: the legalities we need to discuss can be mutually contradictory.

It makes sense to divide this section into two halves: first, there are the legal rights and protections that you enjoy irrespective of whether you are dealing with the media; secondly, there are the specific protections that apply to media contact. The latter arise out of, and are additional to, the former. Both may usefully be addressed following the complaints procedure set out in the previous section above.

But let's start with an overview. For the purposes of this chapter, the key statement of your rights is to be found in the European Convention on Human Rights. This was made binding in UK law in October 2000. It states that every person has the right to a private life and a private family life, and it goes on to state that this privacy extends to every person's correspondence as well as home, health, et cetera. However, what makes this problematic is that the same convention also states that everyone has a right to freedom of expression. You therefore have a right to a private life, but the rest of us have a right to talk about you.

Other potential complications include the UK's Protection from Harassment Act 1997, Data Protection Act 1998, Financial Services and Markets Act 2000 and Communications Act 2003, alongside such Euro-contributions as the Television Without Frontiers Directive.

Note: A "Directive" is still subject to discussion and possible amendment before it is adopted into EU member states' national law as a legally binding "Convention".

There is some discussion in Euro-circles about removing all the complexities of media law by the simple expedient of issuing a further Directive that brings together and resolves all the previous Directives and Conventions, but it may be some time before that sees the light of day.

In the meantime, the situation is being provisionally resolved by the law courts, which have to hear actual cases in which the various rights, et cetera, are tested against each other. A very provisional summary of the current situation may be that the individual's right to privacy is strong, but that the media may succeed in justifying infringements of that privacy where, for example, a public interest is served by the disclosure of private information.

Your right to privacy applies irrespective of whether you are dealing with the media, as do your rights in relation to defamation and libel (as do a range of other rights that are not directly relevant here). In relation to the media, you have a number of additional protections that are detailed in the codes of practice set out and enforced by the Press Complaints Commission (PCC; for print) and Ofcom (for broadcast media). Ofcom's authority over the broadcast media derives from legal statute, while the PCC's code is voluntary. This does not mean that the PCC is necessarily "weaker" than Ofcom, because the print media prefer their voluntary code to the statutory replacement that might be implemented if it proved ineffective. They have an incentive to comply with their code.

We will now move on to examine the relevant provisions of the PCC's and Ofcom's codes of practice. These detail the rights you have specifically with regard to the media's treatment of you, and are additional to your ordinary legal rights in relation to privacy, libel, et cetera. You may expect editors, and most journalists, to be aware of the provisions of these codes.

The Press Complaints Commission (PCC)'s code of practice

This is a selective account which draws heavily on material published at the PCC's website (www.pcc.org.uk). Note that the full code is more comprehensive than this section suggests. A number of provisions (protecting children, for example) have been omitted because they are not relevant here.

Note also that the code favours restitution by publication: editors will tend to be receptive to any suggestion involving published corrections, or apologies, or follow-up pieces putting the facts straight.

The code "both protects the rights of the individual and upholds the public's right to know". It must be honoured "not only to the letter but in the full spirit". It should not be interpreted too narrowly, nor too broadly. Where a publication is criticised by the PCC, it must publish the PCC's adjudication "in full and with due prominence".

Provisions of this code that are relevant to this book include the following:

- **Accuracy**

  Newspapers and periodicals should take care not to publish inaccurate, misleading or distorted material including pictures. Whenever it is recognised that a significant inaccuracy, misleading statement or distorted report has been published, it should be corrected promptly and with due prominence. An apology must be published whenever appropriate.

  Newspapers, whilst free to be partisan, must distinguish clearly between comment, conjecture and fact. A newspaper or periodical must report fairly and accurately the outcome of an action for defamation to which it has been a party.

- **Opportunity to reply**

  A fair opportunity for reply to inaccuracies must be given to individuals or organisations when reasonably called for.

- **Privacy**

  Everyone is entitled to respect for his or her private and family life, home, health and correspondence. A publication will be expected to justify intrusions into any individual's private life without consent. The use of long lens photography to take pictures of people in private places without their consent is unacceptable.

  Note: Private places are public or private property where there is a reasonable expectation of privacy.

- **Harassment**

  Journalists and photographers must neither obtain nor seek to obtain information or pictures through intimidation, harassment or persistent pursuit. They must not photograph individuals in private places without their consent; must not persist in telephoning, questioning, pursuing or photographing individuals after having been asked to desist; must not remain on their property after having been asked to leave and must not follow them.

- **Listening devices**

  Journalists must not obtain or publish material obtained by using clandestine listening devices or by intercepting private telephone conversations. [More on this later in this chapter.]

- **Misrepresentation**

  Journalists must not generally obtain or seek to obtain information or pictures through misrepresentation or subterfuge. Documents or photographs should be removed only with the consent of the owner. Subterfuge can be justified only in the public interest and only when material cannot be obtained by any other means.

- **Discrimination**

  The press must avoid prejudicial or pejorative reference to a person's race, colour, religion, sex or sexual orientation or to any physical or mental illness or disability. It must avoid publishing details of a person's race, colour, religion, sexual orientation, physical or mental illness or disability unless these are directly relevant to the story.

- **Financial journalism**

  Even where the law does not prohibit it, journalists must not use for their own profit financial information they receive in advance of its general publication, nor should they pass such information to others. They must not write about shares or securities in whose performance they know that they or their close families have a significant financial interest without disclosing the interest to the editor or financial editor.

  They must not buy or sell, either directly or through nominees or agents, shares or securities about which they have written recently or about which they intend to write in the near future.

- **Confidential sources**

  Journalists have a moral obligation to protect confidential sources of information.

Ofcom's code of practice

This is a selective account which draws heavily on material published at Ofcom's website (www.ofcom.org.uk). Note that the full code is more comprehensive than this section suggests. This is because Ofcom's remit extends beyond the protection of those dealing with the broadcast media, into such activities as promoting media literacy. Ofcom does not regulate audio-visual or other material delivered via the internet, although its published material acknowledges that the internet is changing audience expectations.

Ofcom's approach to regulation is based on the premise that "freedom of expression is at the heart of any democratic state" and that "broadcasting and freedom of expression are intrinsically linked." Ofcom's focus is on "adult audiences making informed choices within a regulatory framework which gives them a reasonable expectation of what they will receive."

In the protection it extends to those dealing with the broadcast media, Ofcom focuses on fairness and privacy. It also regulates whether commercial references can be made in a broadcast. For each of these areas of concern, it states a principle, and then a rule, and then a series of practices to be followed.

To deal first with **fairness**, the principle is:

  To ensure that broadcasters avoid unjust or unfair treatment of individuals or organisations in programmes.

And the rule is:

> Broadcasters must avoid unjust or unfair treatment of individuals or organisations in programmes.

Among the practices to be followed are the following. **Broadcasters should:**

- **Deal fairly with contributors and obtain informed consent**

  Broadcasters and programme makers should normally be fair in their dealings with potential contributors to programmes unless, exceptionally, it is justified to do otherwise.

  When a person is invited to make a contribution to a programme (except when the subject matter is trivial or their participation minor) they should normally, at an appropriate stage: be told the nature and purpose of the programme; be told what kind of contribution they are expected to make; be informed about the areas of questioning and, wherever possible, the nature of other likely contributions; be made aware of any significant changes to the programme as it develops; and be given clear information, if offered an opportunity to preview the programme, about whether they will be able to effect any changes to it.

- **Give proper consideration of facts**

  Before broadcasting a factual programme, including programmes examining past events, broadcasters should take reasonable care to satisfy themselves that: material facts have not been presented, disregarded or omitted in a way that is unfair to an individual or organisation; and anyone whose omission could be unfair to an individual or organisation has been offered an opportunity to contribute.

  If a programme alleges wrongdoing or incompetence or makes other significant allegations, those concerned should normally be given an appropriate and timely opportunity to respond. Where a person approached to contribute to a programme chooses to make no comment or refuses to appear in a broadcast, the broadcast should make clear that the individual concerned has chosen not to appear and should give their explanation if it would be unfair not to do so.

  Where it is appropriate to represent the views of a person or organisation that is not participating in the programme, this must be done in a fair manner.

- **Avoid deception, set-ups and 'wind-up' calls**

  Broadcasters or programme makers should not normally obtain or seek information, audio, pictures or an agreement to contribute through misrepresentation or deception. (Deception includes surreptitious filming or recording.) However, it may be warranted to use material obtained through misrepresentation or deception without consent if it is in the public interest and cannot reasonably be obtained by other means.

Turning now to **privacy**, the principle is:

  To ensure that broadcasters avoid any unwarranted infringement of privacy in programmes and in connection with obtaining material included in programmes.

And the rule is:

  Any infringement of privacy in programmes, or in connection with obtaining material included in programmes, must be warranted. If the intrusion is warranted because it is in the public interest, then the broadcaster should be able to demonstrate that the public interest outweighs the right to privacy.

Among the practices to be followed are the following. **Broadcasters should:**

- **Respect private lives, public places and legitimate expectation of privacy**

  Legitimate expectations of privacy will vary according to the place and nature of the information, activity or condition in question, the extent to which it is in the public domain (if at all) and whether the individual concerned is already in the public eye. Private behaviour can raise issues of legitimate public interest.

  When people are caught up in events which are covered by the news they still have a right to privacy in both the making and the broadcast of a programme, unless it is warranted to infringe it. This applies both to the time when these events are taking place and to any later programmes that revisit those events.

  Any infringement of privacy in the making of a programme should be with the person's and/or organisation's consent or be otherwise warranted.

  If an individual or organisation's privacy is being infringed, and they ask that the filming, recording or live broadcast be stopped, the broadcaster should do so, unless it is warranted to continue.

  When filming or recording in institutions, organisations or other agencies, permission should be obtained from the relevant authority or management, unless it is warranted to film or record without permission. Individual consent of employees or others whose appearance is incidental or where they are essentially anonymous members of the general public will not normally be required.

- **Use appropriate methods to gather information, sound and/or images**

    The means of obtaining material must be proportionate in all the circumstances and in particular to the subject matter of the programme.

    Broadcasters can record telephone calls between the broadcaster and the other party if they have, from the outset of the call, identified themselves, explained the purpose of the call and that the call is being recorded for possible broadcast (if that is the case) unless it is warranted not to do one or more of these practices. If at a later stage it becomes clear that a call that has been recorded will be broadcast (but this was not explained to the other party at the time of the call) then the broadcaster must obtain consent before broadcast from the other party, unless it is warranted not to do so.

    Surreptitious filming or recording should only be used where it is warranted. Normally, it will only be warranted if: there is prima facie evidence of a story in the public interest; and there are reasonable grounds to suspect that further material evidence could be obtained; and it is necessary to the credibility and authenticity of the programme.

As to **commercial references**, the principle is:

    To ensure that the independence of editorial control over programme content is maintained and that programmes are not distorted for commercial purposes [and] to ensure that the advertising and programme elements of a service are clearly separated.

And the rule is, not surprisingly:

    Broadcasters must maintain the independence of editorial control over programme content [and] broadcasters must ensure that the advertising and programme elements of a service are kept separate.

What this means is, sadly, that broadcasters are legally prohibited from plugging your products on air. Practices not to be followed include these:

- Products and services must not be promoted in programmes.

- No undue prominence may be given in any programme to a product or service.

- Product placement is prohibited.

Sorry.

More on recording devices

As both the PCC and Ofcom make clear, journalists are prohibited from publishing information obtained by the use of clandestine recording devices. It is not illegal to record face-to-face interviews or telephone conversations, but the principle is that all parties should be aware that they are being recorded/filmed. Therefore, you should expect to be notified if a journalist is intending to use a recording device in an interview with you, and you should disclose your own use of any such device. But this is a guideline; no law is being broken when a journalist records/films you in an interview.

Be aware, however, that journalists always record interviews and don't always bother to disclose this. There is a widespread assumption (with no legal basis) that acceptance of recording devices is implicit in the agreement to be interviewed. In practice, assume that you're being recorded unless you're advised otherwise – and even then, don't be too sure. A media interview is never a private conversation.

Perhaps a more useful piece of advice might be: don't trust technology. As every journalist knows, landline mouthpieces and mobiles can transmit every sound in a room and most of the sounds in the adjacent corridor. It is strangely easy to think that you've put a journalist on hold, when in fact they're still able to hear everything said. And putting your hand over the mouthpiece just makes what you're saying more interesting.

Jigsaw identification

This doesn't appear in the accounts of the PCC's and Ofcom's codes of conduct above, but it matters. You might have legitimate grounds for complaint if you are the victim of "jigsaw identification".

In circumstances where you feature anonymously in media coverage – you've gone off the record, for example – you might be identifiable via any "jigsaw pieces" that are included in the write-up. "That's nonsense," says our anonymous source, tugging at his beard. If you're the only bearded anonymous source in the industry, expect trouble.

This might not be an over-serious consideration, but if you're going off the record, even with a journalist you know, make sure, first, that it's understood you really, really don't want to be identified, and secondly, that there's no reason why the journalist might want to identify you.

What is an injunction?

If you've said something you shouldn't have said, this might be worth knowing.

An injunction is a legal mechanism whereby a person may be legally prevented from carrying out an action.

An injunction may be used to prevent publication of sensitive information, while an "emergency injunction" may achieve this result at short notice.

Note: An injunction will only be valid after it has been served on the person to whom it applies; such service should be carried out by a lawyer.

You may apply for an injunction through your solicitor, or directly to a County Court or Magistrate's Court, or in some cases to the High Court. You will have to make a statement justifying your application, which may be challenged by the other party. In the case of an emergency injunction, that challenge may be heard at a subsequent hearing; the injunction may be granted and then subsequently lifted.

And finally ... useful websites

These are the bodies that hear specifically media-related complaints:

* The Press Complaints Commission (PCC) may be found at www.pcc.org.uk and covers the print media.

* Ofcom (The Office of Communications) covers the broadcast media and may be found at www.ofcom.org.uk.

The BBC offers guidance on how to complain to the BBC at www.bbc.co.uk/complaints. After you've complained directly to the BBC and before you complain to Ofcom, you should take your complaint to the BBC Governors at www.bbcgovernors.co.uk.

Index

A

B